Praise for George A. Aschenbrenner's

Quickening the Fire in Our Midst

"*Quickening the Fire in Our Midst* is on the 'must read' list for diocesan priests, bishops, seminarians, vocation directors, and those involved in seminary work. . . . We have long waited for such an insightful book on diocesan priestly spirituality. The chapters are filled with hope, practical advice, a holistic approach to spirituality—and a call to renewal among us as diocesan priests."

Bishop Gregory M. Aymond, diocese of Austin

"Fr. Aschenbrenner's experience in training diocesan priests and his ministry among them has resulted in his capturing the essentials that characterize the spirituality distinctive to them. . . . This well-focused, insightfully theological treatment should be among the 'musts' for every diocesan priest and for the seminary personnel involved with their formation."

Most Reverend John C. Favalora, archbishop of Miami

"Fr. Aschenbrenner draws on his extensive experience and personal reflection to offer valuable insights into the distinctive identity and spirituality of diocesan priests. Consequently, his writing provides an enriching opportunity to bishops, priests, and seminarians and a helpful resource to those involved in priestly formation, whether before or after ordination. *Quickening the Fire in Our Midst* has the potential of making a significant contribution to the ongoing spiritual renewal of the diocesan priesthood."

Bishop Robert H. Brom, diocese of San Diego

"George Aschenbrenner adds his voice to the growing conversation on spirituality and identity of the diocesan priest. [But] his work takes the conversation to a new and necessary depth, by highlighting the priest's interior life in relationship to all he does. His words give hope to diocesan priests longing to find God's loving presence in the midst of all that distinguishes the particular beauty of this call to holiness."

Reverend Richard J. Gabuzda, director,
Institute for Priestly Formation, Omaha, Nebraska

"Fr. George Aschenbrenner . . . describes in a fresh way the 'fire' of diocesan priesthood and the beauty and challenge of a distinctive diocesan spirituality. . . . This book is a must for anyone discerning a priestly vocation and for all those who assist them. It will challenge both the new seminarian and the men celebrating many years of priestly life."

Most Reverend Robert J. Carlson, bishop of Sioux Falls

"In **Quickening the Fire in Our Midst**, Fr. Aschenbrenner has drawn on long years of experience as a spiritual guide to produce a vivid account of the distinctiveness of the spiritual life of a diocesan priest. . . . This is an intelligent and nuanced book about the strengths and pitfalls of the spiritual journey that marks a parish priest who must be both contemplatively alive and actively evangelical."

Most Reverend Daniel N. Dinardo, bishop of Sioux City

QUICKENING
THE FIRE
IN OUR MIDST

The Challenge of Diocesan
Priestly Spirituality

QUICKENING
THE FIRE
IN OUR MIDST

GEORGE A. ASCHENBRENNER, S.J.

JESUIT
WAY

an imprint of
Loyola Press
Chicago

an imprint of

LOYOLAPRESS.

3441 N. ASHLAND AVENUE
CHICAGO, ILLINOIS 60657

Scripture quotations are from the Jerusalem Bible © by Darton, Longman &
Todd, Ltd., and Doubleday & Company, Inc. 1966, 1967, and 1968. Reprinted
by permission.

The articles reprinted in the appendix originally appeared in *Review for Religious*:
"Consciousness Examen" (January 1972), "A Check on Our Availability: The
Examen" (May 1980), and "Consciousness Examen: Becoming God's Heart for
the World" (November 1988). Permission to use is gratefully acknowledged.

Material previously published in the following articles is presented here in revised
form: "Active and Monastic: Two Apostolic Lifestyles," *Review for Religious*
(September 1986); "Monasticism of the Heart: The Core of All Christian
Lifestyles," *Review for Religious* (July 1990); "Gold Purified in the Fire: Diocesan
Seminary Formation," *Seminary Journal* (winter 1997); "Presumption for
Perseverance and Permanence—A Rudder for Direction and Balance in Priestly
Formation," *Seminary Journal* (spring 1998). Permission to use is gratefully
acknowledged.

Interior template design by Think Design

Library of Congress Cataloging-in-Publication Data

Aschenbrenner, George A.

    Quickening the fire in our midst : the challenge of diocesan priestly
spirituality / George A. Aschenbrenner.

    p. cm.

Includes bibliographical references.

ISBN 0–8294–1948–9 (alk. paper)

    1. Priesthood—Catholic Church. 2. Pastoral theology—Catholic Church.
I. Title.

BX1913.A79 2002

262'.14273—dc21

2001007994

Printed in the United States

02 03 04 05 06 07 08 09 Bang 9 8 7 6 5 4 3 2

For the bishops, priests, and seminarians
who opened their hearts
and revealed the Fire
that makes this book possible.

I will raise up a faithful priest for myself;
he shall do whatever I plan and whatever I desire.

1 SAMUEL 2:35

Table of Contents

Acknowledgments

As this book goes to print, I have the happy task of thanking people who have influenced this final copy. My own Jesuit formation is a foundation without which this book would not have been possible. Over the years, many diocesan priests and seminarians, together with my family and many friends, provided encouragement, at times without any awareness on their part. Four people read the manuscript thoroughly in the midst of their busy lives and offered invaluable suggestions: Bishop Robert Morneau, Dr. Michael Downey, Fr. Richard Gabuzda, and Fr. Michael O'Malley. Their kindly insight marks many parts of this book.

The staff at the Jesuit Center for Spiritual Growth made it possible for me to be away for two and a half months. The secretarial assistance of Geraldine Bean and Diane Ross provided something I could never have done myself. The Jesuit community at Gonzaga High School in Washington, D.C., in providing a home for me that was caring but never intrusive, spurred me on in the long, hard work of writing. The staff of the Institute for Priestly Formation shares the dream of this book. I am also grateful to the people at Loyola Press, from the gracious reception of the manuscript by Fr. George Lane, S.J., to the competent and kind guidance of Linda Schlafer in bringing the project to publication.

Finally, words do not do justice to my gratitude for Joseph Whelen, S.J., a theologian, a poet, and a dear friend whose lovingly honest critiques of my articles over many years have taught me a lot about writing, about words, about carefully nuanced meaning, and about heart, where the inspiration of love lives forever.

Foreword

The Second Vatican Council brought many surprises to those who planned and guided it. So often, carefully crafted, scholarly first drafts of documents encountered criticism as being too removed from the pastoral needs of the Church and too empty of the fire of faith and the living word of God.

These drafts were rewritten in light of the debate, usually at least twice, as the council moved toward consensus. So it was with the Decree on the Ministry and Life of Priests. As a priest witness of the council, I followed the decree's development with a personal interest, for it came to chart a way of living the priesthood shaped for the Church's needs and our own in the latter part of the twentieth century. An early draft spoke of the "Life and Ministry" of the priest. The final document reversed the order: it was to be "Ministry and Life," with priestly spirituality flowing out of ministry.

In these pages, Father George Aschenbrenner, S.J., offers us priests a way into the heart of how that spirituality can and should be lived out today. He examines the particular stresses priests face and describes attitudes and resources essential for maintaining or recapturing priestly joy.

With a compelling blend of practical insight and poetic imagery, Father Aschenbrenner leads the reader to a fresh understanding of what Pope John Paul II describes as the "gift and mystery" of the diocesan priesthood. This fresh understanding reinforces prayer, reminds one of the place of regular self-examination and discernment, and helps all to see that, as the priest experiences personally the unfailing love of Jesus, he is the better prepared to offer a flexible, credible, transforming pastoral love to the people whom he leads and serves.

I read these pages between sessions of the World Synod of Bishops' treating of the bishop as the Servant of the Gospel of Jesus Christ for the Hope of the World. In them I found a practical complement to the abundance of humble and hopeful sharing in the synodal discussions. In this volume is a wisdom distilled from years of offering spiritual direction to diocesan priests and to those preparing for the diocesan priesthood. It speaks as well to bishops, whose spirituality is also rooted in a ministry that flows from ordination.

May the Holy Spirit touch the heart of every priest who reads this book with the grace to find here the light and fire that flow from the heart of the Crucified and Risen Christ Jesus.

Cardinal William H. Keeler
Archbishop of Baltimore
October 28, 2001

The Issue and One Response

In the United States, most dioceses face a continuing decrease in the number of priests available for active ministry.[1] Parishes are being combined and realigned, and priests are often covering two or more parishes. Though some countries in the world are experiencing a rapid increase in diocesan priestly candidates, in the United States the decline in available diocesan priests is a matter of considerable concern. For vocation directors especially, but also for some bishops and personnel boards, it is not a time for self-congratulation.

While not denying the evidence of a growing serious problem, in this book I will consider the diocesan priesthood from a brighter perspective. A horizon enshrouded in the dull gray of a dismal future, at times even lined with thunderously threatening, angry clouds, can give way, with hope and hard work, to a brighter future. The concrete, detailed development of a distinctive spirituality can restore to diocesan priesthood a haunting radiance, a promising attractiveness that resembles the sparkle of flames in a lively fire. This is the central claim of this book. The hope of such a claim is founded on the unique particularity of God's fire of love, aflame for glory in every human heart—and, as a matter of amazing fact, in all of reality.

But I have run a bit ahead of the book's development. We must investigate the issue of this problematic moment in the diocesan priesthood before this book's response can be described and appreciated.

The Issue: Much Concern for an Overextended Priesthood

Many people have decried the present state of the diocesan priesthood, and it has been the object of much negative attention in recent years. A recent book depicts the changing face of the priesthood.[2] An article in *Human Development* claims that "some, taking stock of the declining numbers of priests and the public scandals, have declared that the priesthood is 'rotting' or 'collapsing.' One religious leader spoke of trying to 'hold the diocese together' until vocations pick up."[3] In an article in *America,* Francis Dorff states that "some of the most dedicated priests I know are killing themselves. They are working themselves to death, unable to see any other option. . . . There seems to be no way out. At the same time, there is a deep conviction among many of these dedicated priests that 'something has to give.'"[4] The Cistercian writer Thomas Keating claims that many of the faithful long for the warmth and excitement of the gospel as preached with a fire that is personal and experiential. Such a passionate preaching can satisfy this longing only "if the training of future priests and ministers places formation in prayer and spirituality on equal footing with academic training."[5]

In 1983, Walker Percy, a southern Catholic novelist and essayist, spoke honest, inspiring words to a group of diocesan seminarians who were moving on to the study of theology. "As a Catholic layman, I can only wish you well, for your own sake and for our sake, and express the hope, for good and selfish reasons, that it works out. We need you. I noticed there are not many of you. We are all familiar with the famous shortage of vocations. The statistics are dire." Percy went on to suggest one dimension of the solution to this problematic shortage.

> My own impression, from talking to some of you and your genera-
> tion, is that the *one* place where the answer is not to be found is in
> the relaxation of the standards of the priesthood. It seems to me that
> with the best of you it is exactly the other way around. . . . The best
> of your generation . . . want something else. . . . My impression is that
> your generation is less and less impressed by the easy pitch and more
> and more exhilarated by the singular challenge.

GEORGE A. ASCHENBRENNER, S.J.

A bit later in the same talk he spoke very directly. "I am speaking in particular of the vocation of the parish priest. In my book he is one of the heroes of this age."[6] I share a lot of Percy's conviction.

A burden of mammoth expectations that are often quite unrealistic can push priests to a compulsive working to death. Priests quickly feel, and confront day after day, the challenge and burden of all the encounters and expectations of diocesan service. The daily life of a diocesan priest is not dull. His is surely not a nine-to-five job with strict office hours. While he cannot be on duty twenty-four hours every day, the nature of his vocation is such that he must be available on the front line in the midst of people in their ordinary lives. His daily home cannot be the fortress of a carefully protected rectory or the seclusion of a cabin in the mountains.

Encounters of all sorts fill the priest's day. People come with concerns about the church, their family, their work, and God, concerns that do not find their way onto the table of a doctor or the desk of a lawyer. At times the priest is accused of being authoritarian or of not listening. At other times the cry is for more aggressive leadership. The priest is on display daily at Eucharist and sometimes, on a weekend, celebrates four or more times. In such a variety of encounters, where can he find the wisdom and devotion to know what to say and how to keep his heart in all the sacred words and holy actions that crowd his life?

The diocesan priest's vocation is bathed in confession of all sorts. People confess and expose their hearts to him in intimately personal ways. Despite the human beauty revealed in most of these encounters, the therapeutic health of some of these revelations is questionable. At the same time, the challenge of confessing his own faith and exposing his own heart and relationship with Jesus confronts him every time he preaches and, in fact, in most of the personal encounters of his day. A controlled professional objectivity would be a lot safer, but deep down he knows that this can block the genuine inspiration of his own heart as well as God's touch on people. He sometimes feels submerged, almost to sinking, in the ugly, grimy details of the evil and suffering that drench the lives of his people. Feelings of fatigue and frustration cause him to ask, "Why do they bring all this to me?" Ceaseless suffering and dying, confessed and exposed to him almost daily by his congregation, can have an impact that is deadening and that brings desolation.

To continue in such a vocation can sometimes seem almost impossible. Faithful and zestful service can seem beyond human capability. Keeping one's head above water is not easy, and one does not always feel well-trained for staying afloat in the midst of such a maelstrom of encounters. A man could just sizzle to burnout because of the drudgery of so much routine and repetition conjoined with a requirement of almost infinite availability. Add to these voracious expectations a priest's dawning realization that his spirituality seems irrelevantly vague, theoretical, and piously inadequate, and then the waters threaten to engulf him. When he most needs appreciative understanding, he feels undervalued and ill-equipped, and he often does not know where to turn for help.

One Response: A Distinctive Spirituality

In this book I am not recommending discouragement and frustration, though these feelings are rampant these days in discussions about priestly vocations. The situation surely requires serious reflection and a decisive response, but at a time of tension in the church, this situation can foment its own polarization. A certain concept of priestly formation, when disagreed with in a hardened and simplistic fashion, spawns a sharply divisive reaction in the opposite direction, and at times seminaries are catalogued according to this polarized split. Rather than resolving the situation, battle lines drawn with such determination make the scene even less attractive and compound the problem. Other, more helpful responses are needed. We must surely reflect and pray beyond any polarized position. We must pray to the Lord of the harvest, adapt priestly training to a greater variety of candidates, and increase appropriate vocation promotion.

Yet something additional is also needed. We must look deep into the core of our understanding of diocesan priestly vocation in the church and appreciate anew the unique spirituality of such a priesthood. This approach includes image and strategy but cuts far beyond them. In this book my claim is that both the enormous diversity of expectation laid on diocesan priests and the present decrease in candidates are calling us to face a profound issue of identity. Identity in faith, when clearly perceived, always invokes concern about an appropriate distinctive spirituality, without which such an identity can never catch fire and enliven human hearts to an attractive presence and service in the church. This book describes a distinctive spirituality that is unique to diocesan priesthood. It considers diocesan priestly spirituality in its beauty and its challenge as different from all other spiritualities and vocations in the church. In the face of pessimistic confusion and polarizing tendencies regarding diocesan priesthood, one response more than any other is needed: that a realistic and profound spirituality nourish and inform the distinctive identity that underlies and infiltrates all the dimensions of diocesan priesthood.

When a healthy sense of unique spiritual identity is lacking, another danger can arise. In the face of being so undervalued, some priests wilt and fade away, while others stubbornly assert their clerical superiority. This splinters the situation even more and renders compassionate pastoral service on the priest's part all but impossible. As a human reaction to devaluation, this assertive superiority is predictable, but however understandable this reaction is, it only makes the situation worse. It does not, in my opinion, deal with the foundational need for a distinctive diocesan priestly spirituality.

I have no crystal ball for predicting the future of diocesan priesthood in the United States, much less throughout the world, so this book will not address, much less solve, all the problems of the diocesan priesthood today. Nor will it simply defend the status quo. My aim is simple and yet profound: to root the many aspects of diocesan priesthood in a spirituality that does not create a clerical superiority but does reveal the beauty and distinctiveness of the diocesan priesthood in relation to all other types of Christian identity and service in the church.

Part of acknowledging this distinctiveness is setting the diocesan priesthood off from other forms of witness and commitment in the church. Diocesan priesthood is not the priesthood of Religious Life. When ministerial priesthood is integrated into the life-form of Religious Life, the priestly commitment is influenced and marked by two elements of religious identity: a lifestyle of poverty, celibate chastity, and obedience, and a communitarian attitude and way of life. Without these two essential elements of identity we do not have the life-form of Religious Life, and priesthood focused by these two aspects of religious identity is different from diocesan priesthood. This book will stress the need to develop an attitude of community and a lifestyle of celibate chastity, obedience, and gospel simplicity appropriate to the diocesan priesthood; my concern here is not primarily with priesthood in the Religious life-form.

Nor does my focus concern the admirable state of dedicated laypeople, either single or married. Some laypeople have explicitly committed themselves to singleness through a profession to God of celibate chastity in either a private or a public form. Another growing number of laypeople, who did not originally commit themselves to singleness, now find themselves situated in that lifestyle and are no less serious about their commitment to God. In the dedicated lay, married life-form, God, through the sacrament of matrimony, validates and blesses the call of a man and a woman to live and serve together as husband and wife until death.

Just as each of these lay lifestyles has its own distinctive configuration to Christ, the priest's configuration to Christ has its own unique empowerment. Bestowed through the sacrament of holy orders, the priestly power to call down the fire of the Holy Spirit quickens that same fire of love in our midst and invites us all through our appropriate configuration to Christ to form the universal priesthood of all Christian believers. Baptismal consecration, in its own foundational way, engenders a configuration to Christ and stirs the fire of the Holy Spirit in the heart of the baptized. The glory of God flaming in the church throughout the whole world inspires this diversity and plurality of witness and commitment to Christ. In this book, however, my concern is with the witness and commitment of the diocesan priesthood. As the book progresses, I will develop some of these distinctive differences in more detail.

In approaching the nature of the diocesan priesthood, I will describe in chapter 1 the value of having a distinctive, unique spirituality that enfleshes the ideal of diocesan priesthood. In chapters 2 and 3, I will present a basic distinction of lifestyle that affects all Christian spirituality and a basic rooting of these lifestyles in what I am calling a monasticism of the heart. This foundation, and a profound rooting in God's love alone, happens at the level of identity and can facilitate the availability, flexibility, and mobility that obviously characterize diocesan priesthood. In chapters 4, 5, and 6, I will describe a variety of charisms, or gifts, given by God that constitute the identity and vocation of the diocesan priesthood. In chapters 7 and 8, I will spotlight diocesan priestly preparation, spelling out the important role these charisms play in discerning the presence and the permanence of a call to priestly ordination. In the closing five chapters, I will enlarge on some of the charisms presented earlier that constitute diocesan priestly identity and ministry.

A Sensitive Reading

The book is not a complete treatise on diocesan priesthood, and I am very aware of its limited nature. It is the fruit, however, of many years of experience with diocesan priests and of my prayerful reflection on that experience. I have no doubt that much more can be said on the topic. For this reason, I invite all readers, especially those already living this vocation and those seriously discerning such a call, to be open to the Holy Spirit's inspiration to develop further and in a way uniquely suited to yourselves what is presented here. In this way, the book invites an especially sensitive reading. I hope the reader can leave behind the negative suspicions and criticisms that so often prejudice conversation about diocesan priesthood today. For priests and seminarians, the topic of this book is very personal. Your whole life's energy and vision either are or soon may be involved in this enterprise. The fire of Jesus the High Priest's love and vision must ignite your own daily life of service with him. Nothing merely theoretical and objective will do. So I invite you in a special way to a prayerful reading focused in your own personal relationship with the Risen Jesus. This type of reading will open your heart to stirrings of the Holy Spirit beyond my own words, allowing the book's treatment to grow even as you prayerfully read it.

I must explain why a Jesuit, who obviously is not a diocesan priest, is undertaking this task. I write about a type of ministerial priesthood that is not my own. So I write with an objectivity—and with great admiration and appreciation, too—for this priesthood that is so much in and of the people in their daily lives. My admiration for this priesthood has grown over more than thirty years of working with diocesan priests and seminarians. These years have shown me the problems and the challenges, the weaknesses and the failures, as well as the heroic courage and the faithful generosity of diocesan priests. An overwhelming admiration and respect for diocesan priesthood, therefore, has been giving birth to this book over many years. Finally, as I undertake this project, though I do not write from inside the experience of diocesan priesthood, I do have in common with these my brother priests a bedrock of our ministry: an active, non-monastic spirituality. This will become clear as the book progresses.

Who might be interested in this book? Obviously I hope it will inspire diocesan priests and seminarians. Though I am not writing of the priesthood in consecrated Religious Life, some women and men of that life-form may be interested in this book because they work with diocesan priests. Though the book is not explicitly about the identity and vocation of laypeople in the church, I hope it can be of some interest to them also. I know how eager thousands of laypeople are for the spiritual renewal of the diocesan priesthood. They surmise that the fire of the diocesan priesthood will enkindle the hearts and vocations of the people of God so that, together, we can radiate a love that gives us life and cohesion as it flames a revelation of Christ toward the transformation of our whole universe.

GEORGE A. ASCHENBRENNER, S.J.

CHAPTER 1

A Distinctive Spirituality

The scandal of the particularity of God's love! Lofty, challenging words, yet not beyond our experience, if we reflect a bit. For all of us, at some time or another, a specific awareness of God's love pierces our hearts with a particularity and a uniqueness that takes our breath away. While walking with low, discouraged spirit, I am stopped in my tracks by a cardinal of regal red and pointed crest whose recital of a melodious trill seems just for me. This distraction stops me in amazement, and my spirits begin to shift. That I should be so beautifully greeted in a time of need is wonderful enough. That a loving God is somehow involved invites a further incarnation of my faith. And that this consoling creature be intended with a particularity for me, here and now—seems scandalous, just too incredible to be true. It is a moment of invitation to an especially incarnational faith, and my whole life's personal, intimate relationship with God in the Risen Jesus hangs in the balance. "Why, every hair on your head has been counted. There is no need to be afraid: you are worth more than hundreds of sparrows" (Luke 12:7). This astonishing particularity of God's love takes expression in a unique spirituality for each one of us and for each vocation in the church. This awareness of God's particular love and care for us is also, sad to say, easily blunted by casual complacency, and our daily experience is always dulled by such impersonal unbelief.

Christian Spirituality

Though it is stated dramatically, even scandalously so, the opening of this chapter concerns the foundation of Catholic Christian spirituality. Christian spirituality always focuses on the revelation of God in the promised presence of the Risen Jesus to every human being. This presence is enfleshed in a unique personal relationship that develops over a whole life span. This relationship always presumes the faithful initiative of God, an initiative of love at the heart of God, promised and revealed in the coming of Jesus. Without this initiative of God, no human striving can produce spirituality. And yet, given this essential foundation of God's loving initiative, Christian spirituality always requires the free response of human persons in the grace of the Holy Spirit. Catholic Christian spirituality is, therefore, always Trinitarian and incarnational.

What is seen in Jesus somehow takes flesh in our human hearts. How important it is to recognize and watch in admiration the fire of love growing in Jesus, especially during those early long, hidden years. A fullness of the Holy Spirit, always present in him and native to his divine identity, is like a spark quietly burning to a flame and kindling the energies of his humanity into a special vocation. This fire is contagious in Christian spirituality. Anyone who takes a long loving look at Jesus finds an inner depth, a richness, a fire. To reduce Jesus to a one-dimensional figure is to put a damper on the Holy Spirit, to find someone too plain and Spiritless, whereas anyone seriously contemplating Jesus catches the fire and is drawn into the adventure of Christian spirituality. Without this fire, the enterprise is lifeless and passionless even if intellectually correct. This is not to denigrate the important intellectual element in the balance of Christian spirituality. It is simply to keep the whole torch of our hearts in the full flame of the Holy Spirit, glowing in everything about Jesus.

Much more than a basic philosophy or rationale of any individual's life, Christian spirituality is always radically religious and communitarian. As a Trinitarian experience, the human response is drawn to the God of Jesus in the attractiveness of his own love relationship with the One he called "my dearly beloved Father." This attractiveness of the loving interaction between Jesus and his Beloved is the pull of the Holy Spirit on each of us, luring us into the community of love that is the Trinity. To cling tightfistedly to control of our lives is to resist this magnetic attraction of the Holy Spirit. Such resistance often testifies to blinders fearfully shielding the eyes of our hearts from the radiance of Jesus' own response to the fire of his Beloved's love, a response expressed in daring trust: letting his life fall out of control and into the embrace of all that Love. This love of the Trinity is so real and generously available that it becomes a life we live in faith, if we are capable of a necessary purification. Our response to this Trinitarian invitation reveals the divine hope for community among us all. An individualistic response misses the point, has not really heard the full invitation, and is not authentic Christian spirituality.

Finally, the human response is wholehearted and multifaceted. God's loving invitation registers across the whole spectrum of our being: mind, body, and spirit. Both an overly rational response and an overly emotional response are too narrowly incomplete and, therefore, corrosive of genuine Christian spirituality. We must learn to recognize and integrate the grace stirring on all the dimensions of our human makeup. To escape into one favorite dimension, to live a comfortable, controlled spirituality, is a common temptation for us all. But this always forfeits wholeheartedness, keeps the fire slaked, and belies a genuine Christian spirituality.

In an attempt to integrate the various elements presented in the previous paragraphs, I propose the following as a description of Christian spirituality which I will use throughout the rest of this book: our belief in and response to God's love in Jesus as experienced across the whole spectrum of our human lives so that we may live and serve more and more united with one another and with God in the Holy Spirit.

Distinctive Diocesan Priestly Spirituality

The central point of this book is that diocesan priestly spirituality is a unique version of Christian spirituality. This book, therefore, describes that distinctive Christian spirituality that sets off the diocesan priesthood in its beauty and challenge as different from all other spiritualities and vocations in the church. Describing such a distinctive spirituality can provide a foundation for dealing with some of the challenges facing the diocesan priesthood today.

The existence of a distinctive spirituality for diocesan priests is exactly what many people deny. Even some priests, whose hearts, I surmise, are longing deep down for such a spiritual identity, share this denial. This is not false humility. No, the issue is more serious than that, and this misunderstanding has been prevalent in the church for some time. Benedictines, Franciscans, Jesuits, and other religious congregations do indeed have their own unique spiritualities that somehow flow from the original vision of their founders. Such is not the case for the diocesan priesthood. Nothing special distinguishes that priesthood—or so goes the common misconception. I have often heard this claim from diocesan priests as well as from many other people. It is one of the most serious problems facing diocesan priesthood at this time.

In this book, I beg to differ, in all charity, on a point that is too serious to brook any false humility, misguided kindness, or outright misunderstanding. I surely do not blame any priests for this mistake. It has taken me years of experience with the diocesan priesthood and a lot of prayerful reflection to appreciate the central point this book is proposing: that a spirituality distinctive to diocesan priesthood exists. The lack of appreciation for such a distinctive spirituality always weighs heavily on both the priests themselves and the church as a whole.

When priests do not have a sense of a distinctive spirituality that articulates the unique beauty and value of their priesthood, it is no surprise that a painful and continuing morale problem exists among them.[1] If a diocesan priest does not believe in and appreciate the existence of a unique spirituality that is specific not only to himself but also to the diocesan priesthood as a vocation, he must struggle for basic self-respect. As a result, the fire of the distinctive value of diocesan priesthood cannot inflame any aspect of seminary formation. Even more serious, basic respect within the church as a whole for diocesan priesthood is hardly possible. Msgr. McRae, a former spiritual director at the North American College in Rome, mentioned a joke in a talk he gave to formation personnel. "There was a wonderful priest with whom I worked on a spiritual direction team. He had a sign on his desk that read: 'My job is so secret that not even I know what I am doing.'"[2] We can all laugh at the sign, but we also realize that behind the joke is a very serious issue, one that Msgr. McRae addressed in his talk.

Calling Down Fire

In recent years we have been bashful about describing the unique power of the ministerial priesthood. In the clashing crosscurrents of an overly clerical elitism and a rediscovery of the universal priesthood of all believers, this is understandable. But it has left us with a definition and an image of ordained priesthood that are so common, plain, and colorless that they lack excitement and inspirational value. Fr. Robert Barron, a theologian at Mundelein Seminary, has been trying to change that situation as he teaches and directs seminarians. In an interview about diocesan priesthood,[3] he referred to the Jesuit paleontologist and spiritual writer Pierre Teilhard de Chardin. In his "Mass on the World," Teilhard prays: "empowered by that priesthood which you alone (as I firmly believe) have bestowed on me—upon all that in the world of human flesh is now about to be born or to die beneath the rising sun I will call down the Fire."[4] This divine fire for the transformation of the world is at the core of the two images that Fr. Barron uses for the priest: he speaks of the priest "as one who guides others into the mystery of God and . . . as soul doctor."[5] This fire does not belong to the priest nor, is it of his own creation. It is the fire of God's love in the Holy Spirit, and it is meant to become more and more integral to the life we all lead as baptized disciples of Jesus.

Through ordination, the priest has a unique power to administer that fire, to call it down from heaven, to summon it forth into our midst. In this way the priest is able to doctor that deepest part of the person, which we call the soul. This fire of the Holy Spirit is the transforming and healing power of Christ in our world. Though the priest will make use of a variety of gifts in his ministry, somehow his very presence must continually radiate the vitality of the incarnational fire that underlies everything he does. Such a soul doctor ministers always out of the belief that our deepest hope, joy, promise, and fulfillment are in this fire of the Spirit. The priest stands as a unique minister of that fire.

Calling down the fire in order to lead people into the mystery of God and to doctor the deepest desires of their souls is not limited to the "Mass on the World" but is a power and vision that suffuses the priest's entire life and ministry. This exciting and attractive vision of priesthood sounds a call for serious priestly formation and training. A priest must center his whole being in the fire and learn to mediate it in the midst of busy pastoral settings. This is never easy or automatic, nor is everyone called to this distinctive ministry. This book will develop this vision of diocesan priesthood.

Our God, whose love for each and every one of us is scandalously unique, invites us all to a spirituality of response that is likewise unique. Such a spirituality characterizes each of the variety of vocations in the church. We continue to work at appreciating, developing, and articulating a unique spirituality for each vocation. "Do not be afraid, for I have redeemed you; I have called you by your name, you are mine" (Isaiah 43:1). These words, amazingly, are addressed to each one of us. When applied to a diocesan priest, they not only speak of his individual call but also are true of the diocesan priesthood as a unique vocation in the church that is inflamed by a distinctive spirituality. This book describes the heart of that spirituality.

CHAPTER 2

An Active-Apostolic Lifestyle

Taking a telescopic view of centuries of Christian spirituality is always instructive. Patterns of the human response to God's initiative in Jesus that were not recognized at the time in the concrete situation often stand out in hindsight. The distinction between active spirituality and monastic spirituality has been extrapolated from centuries of experience. This delineation has helped us to appreciate and clarify many contemporary spiritual developments, and it is fundamental to describing a unique diocesan priestly spirituality. In this chapter I will distinguish these two lifestyles and describe diocesan priestly spirituality as active and non-monastic. In the next chapter I will present a monasticism of the heart that must ground the active spirituality and lifestyle of the diocesan priest.

Christian Spirituality: A Difficult Balance

All Christian spirituality is in some way motivated and characterized by an enthusiastic love of Jesus Christ. Over many years, this one, central essence of Christian spirituality has taken expression in many different forms, some of which have at times seemed almost irreconcilable and have proved to be quite misleading. Whenever these different forms are misunderstood and their common grounding in one basic Christian spirituality is forgotten, they can become competitive and can portray themselves as superior to one another. As long as we are careful to maintain our lively familiarity with and genuine belief in Jesus Christ as the foundation of all Christian spirituality, then the active apostolic lifestyle and the monastic lifestyle each stand out as a unique manifestation of the Holy Spirit stirring in human hearts. In the past the Christian tradition has often distinguished between monastic spirituality and apostolic spirituality. I am suggesting a further refinement of that distinction: monastic and active. It is a nuance that seems important as we seek to understand and clarify the basic expressions of Christian spirituality today. I have written about these two lifestyles elsewhere and want to apply them here to diocesan priestly spirituality.[1]

Among the ancient world religions, Christianity is unique in its earthy, incarnational quality. The claim that the Son of God became a full human being is at the very center of the Christian religion. Jesus of Nazareth intimately, precisely, and awesomely enfleshes in our midst the God who lives beyond beginning and end in unapproachable light and holiness. Jesus is not a deceptive illusion or a passing hallucination, but someone who enters our world confidently and profoundly, who lives and loves tenderly, courageously, and thoroughly, yet whose center of identity stretches far beyond this world. His God, addressed so intimately as *Abba,* "dearly beloved Father," focuses Jesus' heart far beyond all of this world.

The God of the Christian religion always far transcends in being, beauty, and life anything of this world. On Calvary Jesus could desire, even choose, an apparently absurd and horrendous death precisely because his identity, though fully lived within this world, is not finally rooted here. This identity is then fully confirmed by God in the blessing of resurrection. Fired by the same Spirit of God, all disciples of Jesus must find their identity in the act of plumbing the depths of God far beyond this world even as they live and love with a profound joy and hope that implicates them seriously within this world. However, it is never an identity limited to what is seen, tasted, or known here and now. This balanced integration of the seriously incarnational with the transcendently eschatological has never been easy for any disciple of Jesus. In the next chapter we will return to this identity as focused in the fullness of God's love beyond the world when we explore the monastic foundation for the diocesan priest's active lifestyle.

Two Different Lifestyles: Always Apostolic

There must never be any doubt about Christianity's healthy, creative, and serious concern for this world. When *being apostolic* means having a serious commitment to and involvement with our world, then it becomes clear that every disciple of Jesus must be intensely apostolic. Not to be apostolic, in this sense, is simply to betray Christian discipleship. For this reason, a facile distinction between apostolic spirituality and monastic spirituality may confuse and mislead. I am proposing that there are two different ways—the monastic and the active—of living out Christianity's serious, apostolic concern for our beautiful, anguished world.

The essential *apostolic* orientation of Christian spirituality can be expressed in *either* a monastic *or* an active lifestyle. These two quite different apostolic lifestyles are the result of God's Spirit at work in the hearts of women and men. This distinction, then, is not something simply of human invention, but derives from ways in which God's love has stirred human hearts through the ages. This distinction between the two dynamics of monastic and active relationship with the world cuts across the whole church, from laymen and laywomen to people in consecrated Religious Life to diocesan priests. To confuse or blend these two distinctive apostolic dynamics is to run the danger of disrespecting God's call in human hearts and of not cooperating in the formation of an appropriate apostolic presence for Christian ministry.

The diocesan priest's appropriate apostolic presence involves the active, non-monastic dynamic, but *active* and *monastic* are not meant as hard-and-fast divisions. Rather they express tendencies, movements of grace in our hearts. The challenge for many Christian disciples is to achieve the proper blend of these two tendencies, an effort that focuses the central issue of the disciple's identity. Spiritual schizophrenia will always result when we attempt an equal balance of active and monastic lifestyles. While many different blends of these two tendencies are possible, either the active or the monastic lifestyle must predominate in order to delineate clearly the spiritual identity of a person or a group. Also, remember that a confused spiritual identity both deadens the heart and weakens the ministry of the priest.

Before we consider the active-apostolic dynamic of the diocesan priesthood, two further reminders are in order. First, no priority of one style is intended. These two lifestyles are different and distinct; one is not superior to the other in any way. Second, in discussing the monastic lifestyle, I will have in mind, for the sake of clarity, its embodiment in the fullness of the appropriate vowed Religious life-form.[2] When seen in such clarity and fullness, the monastic dynamic will stand out much more sharply in contrast to the active dynamic of the diocesan priesthood.

The Active-Apostolic Dynamic of Diocesan Priestly Spirituality

Four aspects of the active-apostolic dynamic give a distinctive contour and orientation to diocesan priestly spirituality and set it apart from the monastic-apostolic dynamic.

1. Ministry is the primary determining influence.

When the active charism is recognized as an essential gift to the diocesan priesthood and to each individual priest, then it is ministerial involvement, rather than formal prayer, that determines the contour and schedule of daily life.

This is an important but very subtle point, requiring further elucidation lest it be seriously misunderstood. By giving primacy of influence to ministry I do not mean to deny the absolute importance of quiet contemplation for busy diocesan priests. Without mature prayer, mature ministry is just not possible. It is very easy for busy priests to slide into a runaway, unfocused rush of daily activities, but how this furthers God's reign of love in the hearts of the people can be highly suspect. Let me be firm and clear in asserting this radical importance of formal prayer in the active dynamic of a busy priest's life. Though ministry is the primary influence in his schedule, without serious regular prayer the whole active dynamic of the priest's life is rootless.

In the monastic-apostolic lifestyle, formal prayer has clear and decisive primacy in the development of the whole way of life. The Liturgy of the Hours, the Eucharist in community, and any further private contemplation comprise formal monastic prayer, and these times of prayer have priority in the daily schedule. They determine not only the schedule but also the very structure of the monastic lifestyle. The heart of the monastic person is primarily and thoroughly rapt in the contemplation of God, and simply everything reveals this primacy.

While the importance of formal prayer is not slackened in the active lifestyle of the diocesan priest, it is the legitimate demands of ministry that form the schedule of the day. When the priest enters a new ministry, he cannot carry with him the priority of a past set time for private prayer, especially when this time now interferes with his availability for the new ministry. To cling to a monastic approach violates the dynamic and grace of the active-apostolic charism.

Rather, the priest must first insert himself into the new ministry and get an honest sense of its reasonable demands (and "reasonable" demands never take twenty-four hours a day; that leads to quick burnout!). Only then can his commitment to regular contemplation determine, in a way that best honors the demands of the new ministry, the specifics of when, where, and how long he will pray each day. For the active priest, then, while not a substitute for regular contemplation, ministry is the primary determining influence in the diocesan priest's whole way of life.

2. Flexibility, mobility, and apostolic availability are central.

In order to respond to the challenges and needs of a busy parish, a diocesan priest needs to have a flexible availability of heart and spirit. The regular monastic routine, scheduled as it is around formal prayer throughout the day, is not possible for the busy priest and should neither be expected nor be seen as better than his own way of life. Since mission and active ministry are so central to the active-apostolic lifestyle of the priest, apostolic availability and mobility of body and spirit are crucial. Any rigidity, stubborn selfishness, or immature insecurity will always corrode the availability and mobility needed for active ministry.

Apostolic availability is a readiness of spirit born of a freedom that is radically fascinated with a loving God's faithful commitment to us. This freedom never perdures perfectly in a weak and sinful human heart, so it must be sought and received repeatedly. The more this precious freedom grows in the priests of a whole presbyterate, the more an availability of spirit allows them to be committed fully to their present ministries while always ready to go wherever God's love might lead them in the future.

A key distinction is needed here to prevent another serious misunderstanding. The realities of availability, flexibility, mobility, solitude, and stability can be viewed in two different, but related, ways: either as profound inner realities of heart or as external expressions of those same interior realities. The five qualities listed above, when viewed as inner realities of heart, would typify spiritual maturity for all disciples of Jesus, whether monastic or active. Each of the five would have a unique motivational role in a life of mature discipleship. When viewed as an external expression, one or another of these qualities, while appropriate for one apostolic lifestyle, would violate the contrasting dynamic. For example, monastic vowed stability would externally interfere with active ministerial mobility, just as inner solitude externalized in a Grand Silence through the night would conflict with the adaptability needed in active ministry. These two practices, while interruptive of active-apostolic presence, are keenly important elements in a monastic disciple's profoundly deepening experience of God. This distinction between inner quality of heart and external expression catches well both the overlapping and the separateness of these two apostolic lifestyles.

3. The prayer of the apostolate is most typical for active spirituality.

The ideal and norm for the practice of prayer in the active life of a priest is best described as the *prayer of the apostolate*. This phrase indicates just the reverse of the monastic ideal of the apostolate of formal prayer. Once again the dynamic is different without signifying any superiority.

Keeping in mind the already-emphasized absolute value of regular contemplation in any serious ministerial life, the typical and more important prayer of the active priest is his distinctively prayerful presence pervading all activity. This presence will always involve the carefully discerned integration of regular formal prayer with a day's busy activity so as to find a dear God whose love gives being and meaning to absolutely everything about the priest's day. This prayer of the apostolate should not be mistaken for that claim and practice that many of us struggled with through the 1960s and 1970s: "My work is my prayer." We now know the heresy of such a claim, even though active people, who would not profess such an ideal, can still easily be pressured into living such a distortion. We have learned again over recent years that for no one does work become prayer unless that person regularly stops working—and prays. Then, and only then, does one's work become another way of praying.

So the prayer of the apostolate is not any simplistic identification of work and prayer. Rather the prayer of the apostolate involves two mutual and integral movements. The first is an appropriate, regular involvement in contemplation, which gradually spills over and renders prayerful everything the person does, says, and is. The second is an involvement in activity that stirs a desire for, and sometimes provides the subject matter of, formal private contemplation. As the priest grows faithful and sensitive to these movements, his prayerful presence develops in the midst of all activity—a presence that is the Holy Spirit of God praying and that reveals those clear signs of the Spirit mentioned in chapter 5 of Galatians: "love, joy, peace, patience, kindness, goodness, trustfulness, gentleness, and self-control."[3]

The dynamics of formal prayer are different for the active and the monastic lifestyles. Confusion of these two ideals can be misleading and frustrating for the active priest who is mistakenly struggling to base his life and ministry on the monastic ideal.

4. There is a unity of mind and heart extending far beyond physical presence.

The understanding and role of community are also affected by the differences between these two apostolic dynamics. In recent years Christian community has been much discussed but not easily accomplished. Often the problem stems from unrealistic expectations rooted in a failure to appreciate the contrasting dynamics of community formation in the active and monastic lifestyles.

Christian community is always founded in a union of minds and hearts, a union primarily focused by a shared faith vision. Though many other elements, such as friendship, similar age, training, and interests, may facilitate a union of minds and hearts, none of these can replace the priority of a genuine communitarian faith vision regularly experienced and appropriately expressed. In the active-apostolic dynamic and, therefore, for busy priests, this shared faith vision does not depend as much on the physical presence of all members to each other as it does in the monastic dynamic. Such a shared, active faith vision, when it is real and genuine, infuses in each priest a specific attitude of sharing and support that perdures beyond any temporary physical presence and is not disrupted by the lack of such presence. However, this communitarian bond is not automatic for busy, active priests, and it is not the effect of any one person's fiat. It cannot be superficially external or limited to pockets of friendship. In my view this sense of community is very much related to the diocesan priest's obedience and thus will be treated more fully in chapter 12.

Although the active charism of diocesan priesthood depends less on the physical presence of its members than does the monastic, this certainly does not mean that physical presence can simply be disregarded in a presbyterate. Decreasing numbers of priests, who are already spread far and wide in large dioceses, can unintentionally move the members of a presbyterate to be less and less physically present to each other and to their bishop. But the danger cuts even deeper. The claim is often heard that for diocesan priests, who are not members of consecrated Religious Life, no sense of community should even be expected, that it is just not part of the vocation of the diocesan priesthood. I surely do not claim that diocesan priests should strive for the community of consecrated Religious Life, and especially not for that of monastic life. I do strongly maintain that it is essential for diocesan priests to search out, appreciate, and realize the genuine sense of community that is appropriate to the active dynamics of their lifestyle. This will encourage the hearts of individual priests and give them necessary support in the witness of their celibate lives. Most important, it will enrich and improve the whole ministry of a presbyterate.

In this chapter I have described all Christian spirituality as apostolic by taking the world as seriously and as passionately as God does in Jesus. This essentially apostolic nature springs from an identity centered in a God whose love and reality stretch far beyond our world. This apostolic orientation to the world can happen in either a monastic or an active dynamic, as animated by the Holy Spirit in human hearts. I have traced four aspects of the active dynamic in the vocation of the diocesan priest. It is easy to see how misleading and frustrating it is when diocesan priests confuse these two dynamics and their quite different expectations, first in seminary formation and then in postordination experience.

In the next chapter I will describe a monastic experience of the heart that shifts one's identity center more thoroughly into God, and then establishes a foundation and focus for the priest's active lifestyle.

CHAPTER 3

God's Love: Alone and Enough

Even when the active lifestyle is appreciated as proper for busy diocesan priests and its dynamic is integrated into daily ministry, it can soon run itself thin in a shallow activism. A radical monasticism of the heart—a stark aloneness with God in Jesus—must serve as bedrock for both the active and the monastic lifestyles.[1] Without such grounding, the two lifestyles are built more on sand than on rock, and they run the risk that Jesus' parable makes clear (see Matthew 7:24–7). In this chapter I will describe this monasticism of the heart as fundamental to the baptismal reannouncement of identity for every Christian. In baptism we are plunged into Jesus, into his dying and rising. A fire is lit, and the glowing coals of that fire spark a whole new life. The draft of our generous cooperation is always required to fan this promised future into flame, for it is only in the ashes of dying that the flame of rising can be enkindled. My chief concern in this chapter, however, is to apply this special monastic experience to the busy, active spirituality of diocesan priests.[2] The integration of the appropriate external, active spirituality with this profound monasticism of the heart makes possible a discerning sensitivity that can transform the busy priest's ministry from a shallow activism into a focused and unified life of service.

When detached from a radical experience of oneself as alone with God, the active and monastic lifestyles become superficial, based primarily on externals. In the previous chapter, while I was concerned with the external expressions that distinguish these two legitimate apostolic lifestyles in the church today, I put special stress on the development of the external, active dynamic as essential to the diocesan priesthood. In this chapter I am more concerned with describing the profound inner purity of heart without which the two lifestyles become superficial, competitive, and even misleading. These two dynamics, when perceived for what they are, allow them an interaction that is enriching in itself and then becomes helpful to anyone who is discerning a vocation to one state of life or the other.

These monastic and active dynamics of external lifestyle must always be profoundly rooted in one and the same experience of being alone with God. I have named this foundational experience "monasticism of the heart." This ontological, psychological, affective monasticism, rooted deep in the heart and beyond any lifestyle, is a core religious experience that must ground the identity of all serious disciples of Jesus Christ. It must serve the same purpose for a diocesan priest. This monasticism of the heart must be carefully distinguished from an external monastic lifestyle. I am not trying to monasticize the diocesan priestly lifestyle. For many priests this monasticized lifestyle has seriously scarred their past. The monasticism of the heart of which I speak anchors Christian identity in an experience of God that is far beyond anything of this world, and it thereby stands forth as the absolutely essential foundation for diocesan priestly spirituality.

Though the Greek word *monos* historically developed some further aspects of the meaning of monasticism, especially along communitarian lines with Eusebius and Augustine into the fourth and fifth centuries, the word's basic meaning continues to signify an aloneness, a solitariness.[3] The experience I am describing is one that strips and purifies, scouring the heart to a radical solitude in and with God. For this reason the phrase *monasticism of the heart,* rather than confusing the issue, seems an appropriate depiction of this experience, presented here as fundamental to diocesan priestly spirituality.

Monasticism of the Heart in Jesus' Calvary Experience

All forms of Christian spirituality are founded on and catch fire in the example and experience of Jesus. In its own unique and distinctive way, the diocesan priesthood also focuses on Jesus the High Priest. Ontologically Jesus always somehow knew, in the radical aloneness of his heart, a union with his "dearly beloved Father," a union beyond any other and never capable of full expression in words. It is important for any serious Christian disciple, and especially for the priest, to trace this radical union as it develops humanly through those long hidden years of Jesus' life. A fire similar to the one that flamed forth in Jesus' heart at his Jordan baptism is enkindled in the priest's heart as he contemplates it in awe. "I have come to bring fire to the earth, and how I wish it were blazing already!" (Luke 12:49). This fire, always quietly ablaze in Jesus' heart, contained a logic and wisdom beyond the normal and natural. It entranced the eyes of his heart with the vision of someone who always seemed so intimately close and yet so far beyond the details, or the sum, of any daily situation.

That Jordan experience confirmed the Beloved's choice of Jesus with a love and favor that extroverted his heart in breathless wonder, prayer, and expectant zeal. All through his life, temptation tested and revealed the depth and durability of that love and favor in the face of this world's threatening, seductive designs. It was clear that in some profound way Jesus was not his own. He was a Son whose being utterly relied on his Father, a Son who was always and only fully at home with that dear Father. In those moments of intimacy and clarity, he knew that his dear Father's love would be enough, come what may. Stripped to that love alone, he knew it would see him through anything in the future. In his public ministry Jesus regularly withdrew for prayer in solitude, times precious to him and key to keeping the fire alive. These times of solitude and prayer were not an escape or unrelated to his busy life. No, it was precisely these times that allowed the fire to flame forth and to guide every day's busy activity. In those times of prayer, his heart experienced the intimacy of that fire and, finally, envisioned life with a preternatural clarity. Beyond voice or word, he knew that the Love of his Father was so awesome and always in his favor that it would be enough, whatever the future held.

GEORGE A. ASCHENBRENNER, S.J.

In Jesus' Calvary experience this solitary rootedness in God alone stood forth in stark truth and beauty. At the Last Supper, on the night before he died, Jesus was seized by a moment of special, explicit awareness, as John's Gospel records it: "Jesus knew that the Father had put everything into his hands, and that he had come from God and was returning to God" (John 13:3). It was the awareness of a man who had decided, in the face of opposition that had hardened into the decision to kill him, to enter the darkness of threatened death and to stand lovingly and firmly for the truth—something to which the ministry of his whole life had led him, and now simply demanded of him. He could not, he would not, back off the issue, an issue that was surely more than something worldly, more than some question of human success or the defense of some human ideology. Though it would have enormously important repercussions for the whole world, the issue reached far beyond that immediate situation.

In washing his disciples' feet, that gesture of perfect love (John 13:1), Jesus symbolized the meaning of his whole past life and, even more, of his coming final experience on Calvary, when he would be lifted beyond any point of return. In an olive grove, strengthened by a fearful, anguished renewal of obedient abandonment into the providential, loving hands of his Beloved, Jesus literally gave himself over into the hands of his adversaries. For a moment in that olive grove, the prospect of imminent death struck savagely and violently at the sensibleness of human reason. No temporal cause or rationale, no human ideology brought saving significance into that moment's temporary absurdity. Only a dearly Beloved's love and a mission transcending all ages and boundaries brought light into such darkness. It was a logic and love beyond anything of this world that was able to see through such absurdity.

The starkest and most dramatic experience of utter reliance on God alone occurs at the height of Jesus' Calvary experience. After being stripped of his clothes and lifted on the cross, a last, far starker stripping occurred. Having always been energized by his dearly Beloved's favor and choice, Jesus now felt forsaken and, at the level of *felt experience,* utterly separated from that Beloved who had always been there for him. At the profoundest level of *being* the Son, however, he remained more than ever united to God as the only Son of a dearly faithful Father. In that moment of final, intense testing, Jesus believed in, reclaimed, and confirmed the unimaginable faithfulness of his Beloved Father, which had always been central to his identity. Since it was absolutely all he had left in that moment of apparent forsakenness, Jesus' true and only home stood out dramatically.

With his identity centered in God and far beyond any logic or promise of this world, Jesus crucified does not damn or deny the reality of our world. From the deepest composure of his heart, focused wordlessly on his dearly Beloved, Jesus announced with rocklike hope: "In God alone there is rest for my soul. . . . Rest in God alone, my soul! He is the source of my hope" (Psalm 62:1, 5). That hope, beyond any sensible, felt experience, was blessed by his dear Father with the response of resurrection. This victory of God in the heart of Jesus on Calvary, which stripped and purified him of any ultimate reliance on an earthly hope, is not some escape or turning away from the world. Rather the glorious victory consummated in the Crucified One is a saving mystery of renewed life, love, and hope stretching limitlessly throughout the universe and into the fullness of time. It is an eruption of the Holy Spirit flashing a renewed fire of freedom and enthusiasm into human hearts for the renewal of the whole universe.

Though it is never easy to remain long enough in contemplation of the mystery of Calvary, Christian women and men of all ages have found consolation in that radical simplicity and aloneness, at times to their great surprise. Beyond the fright of such cruel suffering resonates a consolation that can withstand any and all trials in life. Christian piety always focuses on contemplation of the cross, and all its generous service radiates from that profound and faithful center of identity.[4]

Monasticism of the Heart: Essential Foundation for Diocesan Priesthood

The experience described here as a monasticism of the heart underlies Christian commitment of every sort. Thus it plays a foundational role in the distinctive spirituality of the diocesan priesthood. This monasticism of the heart, rather than being established in one specific experience, is an orientation in faith whose development takes time. As a foundational dynamic essential to Christian discipleship, it always shakes any previous identity and establishes a new person in Christ. This developing dynamic, this fundamental orientation in faith, cannot be bypassed in diocesan priestly spirituality without forfeiting qualities that are essential to priestly ministry: durability, faithfulness, and hope-filled joy. The development of this dynamic in faith is never automatic; it requires a choice of cooperation and effort on our part. This costly investment requires the radical conversion of our whole person.

This choice and conversion are initiated and empowered in baptism and stretch over a whole lifetime. A radical reannouncement of identity, proclaimed in baptism, lays the foundation for diocesan priestly spirituality. In chapter 7, we will see the central role that this identity plays in diocesan seminary formation. Within our baptismal faith and always inviting us beyond ourselves is a stark matter to be decided: *either* a God whose love conquers all absurdity *or* a world whose beauty is, in and of itself, absurdly chimerical and unpredictable. Either . . . or. Such a choice is not primarily a matter of our own effort. It is a choice revealed and made for us and with us in the graced beauty of Jesus Christ, especially in his Calvary experience. Jesus himself has made this choice not just for himself but also for each of us. It is a choice of God alone, a love far beyond all other loves, a love that alone fully satisfies our restless hearts.

Though this choice is primarily made for us in Jesus Christ, it is a choice that must be confirmed by a fundamental reannouncement of identity in faith on the part of the diocesan priest. Baptism, as it initiates in our hearts this monastic experience of God alone, involves in some careful, real way a renunciation of this world, with all its goodness and all its allurements—precisely a renunciation of the world as our identity center. As baptized we stand in Christ, identified finally and fully in God alone. Only God's love in Christ, creatively and faithfully burning into the fullness of time, provides ultimate assurance.

Diocesan priestly spirituality builds on this radical reannouncement of identity. In its own distinctive way it involves a renunciation of this world as the center of identity. Through an ongoing, graced, expansive experience of God's love, a whole shift of an individual's center of gravity occurs. Gradually more and more identified in God's love alone, the priest experiences a certain disengagement from the world as an identity center—precisely because he is so fully engaged with the fire of God's love.

To have our identity stretched beyond our selfish limits and into the fullness of God's faithful love and, therefore, to renounce the world as our identity center is not to lose the world. Rather it reveals a whole new vision of the world, as belonging to God, as redeemed in the mystery of Christ, and with the Holy Spirit daily struggling to radiate the fire of God's reconciling love within the infinite variety of human affairs. Diocesan priests, alight with that fire of God's love in the quiet intimacy of their hearts, will find their daily ministry to be part of that radiant daily struggle of the Holy Spirit. Any diffident suspicion of the world is transformed, therefore, in the enlightening love radiating from the heart of the crucified Christ, fully abandoned to his Beloved and blessed in the gift of resurrection. To contemplate Jesus on the cross is not, finally, to hold back but to be inflamed in the mission of the Spirit. Jesus' words in the Gospel of John become a realized prophecy and issue a clarion call of enlightened, confident zeal: "Now sentence is being passed on this world; now the prince of this world is to be overthrown. And when I am lifted up from the earth, I shall draw all men to myself" (John 12:31–2).

At this point a priest may wonder: Am I capable of such an experience? Obviously he must answer this for himself, but some comments are in order. This experience, as mentioned above, is the original blessing of baptism, and God always desires for that grace to deepen and flower. The development and further refining of this grace should also play a central role in any program for priestly formation. Once this experience of monasticism of the heart has taken effect profoundly enough in a priest's life, two further questions surface: How can I keep this experience alive, and What are some of the practical results in my life that demonstrate the liveliness and effectiveness of this experience? Answers to these two questions bring this chapter to a close.

Once abandonment to God's faithful love alone has forged a deep peace in a priest's heart, the concern then quickly arises of how to keep such a foundational experience and attitude alive and operative. It is the natural inclination of our hearts for this special availability to fade over time, and in its fading, not only do our hearts begin to shrink, but the consequences of this experience of abandonment to God alone also begin to dim. Though it is the very nature of our human hearts to long for self-transcendence through self-abandonment, we all know the strong, insidious tendency to live a more predictable life, controlled and even determinedly constricted by selfish, easily rationalized personal preference and prejudice.

For this reason a diocesan priest will need the regular reflection of the consciousness examen,[5] whereby he can carefully observe the contours of his heart, renew in gratitude the expansiveness of God's love for him, and honestly repent of limited responses to such love in the specific details of his day. Such reflection will keep the priest sensitive to those concrete moments in his loving service of others in which God invites him to a renewed surrender beyond himself, a surrender that always extroverts his heart in loving, confident reliance on Jesus Christ. God's love always invites us to step beyond narrow, self-defined limits, and a priest needs regular reflection to notice these invitations.

Daily Eucharist, celebrated reverently and in deep faith, also provides a regular, awesome opportunity to renew the monasticism of the heart. Jesus, through the priest, daily gathers the people at the Last Supper and serves them on the summit of Calvary. Eucharist places the priest and his fellow believers at the center of all time and within the fullness of all reality in Jesus' full-hearted, self-emptying response to the love of his Beloved. Eucharistic love is judgment; it tears the curtain from our hearts and stretches our heart's love to the lengths of God alone and to the breadth of divine care for this world. Such a regular experience of God's infinitely expansive love does not result in the priest's overlooking the daily concerns of a parish. Rather, by restoring the priest and the people to an enlarged perspective, it allows them to inhale a hope that is renewing and both relaxing and inspiringly energetic.

Renewed in Solitude

Without a doubt, the most important means, under God's grace, by which a priest can renew and maintain the monasticism of his heart is regular time alone in the quiet solitude of God's love. In this experience of solitude with God, whether in a protracted daily time of personal prayer, or in a monthly hermitage day, or in an annual silent retreat, or in some other regular time of quiet recollection, the issue is always the same: to stop all busy activity and just *be,* alone, in the profound peace and quiet of God's love. Most often this is not easy but calls the priest up short and shakes him free of life's many urgent concerns so as to expose and renew the one truly important reality in life: full, trusting obedience to God's saving love in Jesus.[6] In *The Way of the Heart,* Henri Nouwen calls solitude the necessary furnace of transformation whereby the minister's compulsion burns more and more to compassion.[7] This scorching purification of his many compulsions burns its way patiently and gradually into the deep center of the priest's heart, where he stands, lives, and breathes, in the fire of love, with God alone. In this way solitude confronts diocesan priests and invites them, beyond any introvert-extrovert distinction, to a monasticism of the heart, which roots their identity in the Trinity of God at a depth of heart beneath all active or monastic external lifestyles.

Results

This monastic experience produces clear signs of the liveliness and effectiveness of a profound rooting of the priest's heart in God's love alone. Some of the resulting qualities seem in short supply today in the diocesan priesthood and throughout the church in general. In the face of undeserved and unexplained suffering, of bitter and revengeful hatred, of unjust and enslaving poverty, apostolic hope, joy, and enthusiasm seem naively unrealistic, if not absolutely impossible. Disillusionment and a despondency verging on angry despair are understandably in the hearts of many busy priests. Only a priest profoundly rooted and ultimately identified in God's love beyond all other loves becomes enlightened enough to recognize God's suffering, saving love at work in his immediate circumstances. He then becomes free and faithful enough to commit himself to God's passionately loving justice, which is always and only revealed in the mystery of Christ crucified to the fullness of resurrection. This formative experience and vision, essential for one who doctors souls, burns into the priest a fire that is unquenchable and hope, joy, and enthusiasm that are indefatigable, whatever may happen. The lack of such qualities will always limit the church's missionary response to specific critical needs. Even worse, it will corrupt and gainsay the witness of diocesan priests to the Good News of a God whose love has a power to save and transform beyond the interference of any worldly power.

Through this profound monastic experience and orientation, contraries become integrated in a new balance of tension. Light and darkness, life and death, success and failure, just and unjust situations, a parish I like and one for which I seem not very fitted—none of these, nor any of countless other alternatives for the priest, become either-or choices about God's loving presence. Rather, they become both-and situations, each action capable of revealing the mystery of God's universally saving love in Christ. The fire of such an insightful and extensive vision is available only to generous, prayerful, apostolic priests—pacified and strengthened, surely, in the support of one another but finally in a hope against hope about God's love alone. Without a genuine monasticism of the heart, however, such insightful apostolic vision, enthusiastic freedom, unquenchable fire, and irrepressibly joyous hope are simply not possible. The courage of human willpower alone is not even an issue here. Rather the issue is faith—faith acted out as relationship—a faith that can move the mountains of disbelief in our own hearts and can reveal to those chosen the fire of God's superabundant love burning strong in our weakness.

This deep-hearted monastic experience, as it strips priests' hearts more and more of prejudice and excessive self-defense, will reveal the fire of God's love glowing everywhere in everything. A God whose saving love is unquestionably at work in all things can actually be found in all things, but only by the priest who is faithfully purified in the experience of the *monos*—that experience of being with God alone and somehow knowing that the fire of that love is *enough,* come what may. For this priest, then, all life, however plain, humdrum, or even incongruous, becomes religious experience. The sacred-secular split in a priest's experience that often saps the energy of his heart can thus be healed in an integration that discovers and focuses God's loving grace and finds a body for God's Spirit, present in all human experience.

Conclusion

The diocesan priestly active lifestyle requires the necessary foundation of what I am here calling monasticism of the heart. Besides undergoing appropriate preparation in a formation program, priests need to recognize contemporary invitations to this monastic experience—a monasticism that roots a priest in Jesus Christ and without which the diocesan priestly active lifestyle cannot escape fragmentation, rootlessness, and that final disappointment that simply must come to any life whose ultimate identity, in its depth and solitude, is not the indwelling Trinity of God alone.[8] This profound monasticism speaks at once to all diocesan priests of a number of realities: the radiant fire of a dear God's love, which is beyond all earthly imagining; the restless fire of longing in all our hearts, never ultimately satisfied in this world; and, finally, the saving mystery of Christ passionately aflame in the Spirit and eager to forge all our energies for the incandescent renewal of the whole universe into the fullness of time.

This monastic foundation for diocesan priestly spirituality is so important that it will serve as a backdrop for the rest of this book. In the next three chapters I will sketch, with some concrete detail, a picture of the diocesan priesthood, whose lively distinctive spirituality is the central concern of this book.

CHAPTER 4

Identity and Territory

The active and monastic dynamics, as different as they are, catch fire in Christian spirituality insofar as they are rooted in the ongoing experience of a monasticism of the heart. Appreciating the dynamics of an active lifestyle as springing from a monasticism of the heart provides an essential foundation for this book's description of a spirituality that is distinctive to diocesan priests. In these next three chapters I will describe a composite of many charisms that forms a working description of diocesan priesthood in its uniqueness as we know it in North America at this time. These identifying charisms comprise a multifaceted, distinctive spirituality for diocesan priesthood as well as a unique diocesan priestly identity. They cannot simply be reduced to a list of functions or a litany of priestly activities without paying a costly price. Carl Arico reminds priests that "we reduce our call to function. No matter how sublime that may be, functions are still functions. They do not give identity."[1] I will not develop each of the charisms at length, lest the book's size become unwieldy. I will develop a few of them at greater length as examples of the spirituality that is contained in each of the charisms. In this way, again, I invite the reader to carry on the book's further development.

Before I begin to sketch a picture of diocesan priesthood, some clarifying introductory comments are in order. First, the word *charism* can have confusing connotations. I use the word here in the straightforward sense of a gift given by God. It is not a gift given to everyone, nor can it be gained solely by human striving. Of course the gift must be received, intentionally acknowledged, and developed by hard effort. My use of the word does not connote its ordinary meaning as used in congregations of consecrated

Religious Life. Nor do I intend the word to imply the charismatic as distinct from the institutional and hierarchical aspects of the church. In my use of the word I will be describing an integration of many gifts that God gives as evidence of a call to diocesan priesthood.

Second, these charisms could also be reduced to the traditional three dimensions of the mission of Jesus: prophetic, priestly, and royal. Since Vatican II, it has been clear that all baptized disciples of Jesus share this threefold mission. In describing a rather large number of charisms, however, I am able to be more specific and concrete in my sketch of diocesan priesthood.

Third, none of these many charisms, by itself, catches the distinctiveness of this priesthood. It is precisely in the composite that the appropriately distinctive identity and spirituality of diocesan priesthood are revealed.

Fourth, though I have gathered these charisms into groups with a certain logic, there is nothing infallible about this lineup. It could be done in another way. As I mentioned earlier, this sketch of diocesan priesthood will continue to develop. Further touches of the brush, I am sure, will add even more specificity to the picture. This is a work in progress, and it is my hope that readers inspired by the Holy Spirit will discuss new charisms and further develop some of the ones presented here.

1. An Ordinary Priest in the Midst of Common, Ordinary People

In his book *Pastoral Presence and the Diocesan Priest,* Fr. Paul Keyes relates an encounter he had with a cook in St. Paul's Passionist Monastery in Pittsburgh while he was studying at Duquesne.[2] Thinking he was a Passionist priest from Boston, the cook asked Fr. Keyes if he knew a number of priests in the Boston area. Finally, after he confessed to being a secular priest, she said, "Oh, I'm sorry . . . you are just one of those 'ordinary' priests." Then she became embarrassed and apologized for such a description. Fr. Keyes came to realize that she had not insulted him but had paid him a great compliment by calling him "just an ordinary priest." As he reflected on this encounter, Fr. Keyes came to appreciate "the great dignity there is in being a priest who lives intimately in the life and concerns of common, everyday people."[3] The diocesan priest does not usually work with special clienteles, such as college or high school students or missionary people in foreign lands, as is often true of priests of consecrated Religious Life. "To be an ordinary priest carries the great dignity and responsibility of being called by Christ to live or dwell near ordinary people in their common, everyday, spiritual, and temporal needs."[4] In this way the diocesan priest lives in the midst of the great mixture workers, students, nurses, the elderly, the unemployed: right in the middle of this mix of humanity is where his priesthood inserts him. Rather than being an insult or a humiliation, being an ordinary priest in the great mix of common people in a certain locale announces the healing presence of someone who doctors people's souls by guiding them into an encounter with mystery— the mystery of the purifying fire of God's saving love.

2. Always on Call on the Front Line

In his book, Keyes refers to a fellow diocesan priest's comment: "We are constantly on the front line."[5] This availability is another part of the diocesan priesthood's attraction. It also necessitates its own challenging transformation. As if equipped with a pager for the Holy Spirit, the priest resounds in the midst of the people, not with an interruptive static, but with the welcoming accessibility of God's love. Who will be on the other end of the latest ringing phone or doorbell? The answer to that question is usually unpredictable and often charged with surprise. This availability on the front line prevents much sense of protection or shelter from all sorts of calls on the priest's time and person. This challenge is balanced with the attractiveness of making God present in the healing balm and power of Jesus' love for one and all in an almost infinite variety of situations. This priestly presence flickers constantly and invitingly like a candle in the window for all passersby.

Diocesan priests also learn quickly that they cannot be available twenty-four hours of every day. Setting reasonable limits will enhance and intensify the quality of their availability rather than compromise it. Because such availability is essential, the concrete expression of it must be carefully discerned when integrated with other values, such as, for example, the support of priests in a rather large area living together. To honestly weigh the support of each other against a potential availability to the ordinary people of a particular area is not easily done, but it is central to preserving this charism of diocesan priesthood.

This availability on the front line enlivens the pastoral charity that Pope John Paul II in *Pastores Dabo Vobis* sees as the priest's very identity, not just something he occasionally does. "It is not just what we do, but our gift of self, which manifests Christ's love for his flock. Pastoral charity determines our way of thinking and acting, our way of relating to people. It makes special demands on us."[6] The expression of this pastoral charity runs the gamut from a prophetic stance for justice in the local community to a cheerful visit in a nursing home to a compassionate visit to a family grieving the death of a parent and on into an almost infinite variety of situations. This pastoral charity is never fulfilled in a pro forma protocol. Only the genuine presence of the priest's very person, as the embodiment of the healing fire of God's love, will do.

If a priest's pastoral presence is to embody the compassion of Jesus, a basic humility must suffuse his pastoral charity. Both religious experience and basic human experience, when underdeveloped, will short-circuit the priest's pastoral effectiveness. Without a profoundly personal experience of God's unique love for him and without a profound self-knowledge and self-acceptance, the heart of the priest can unconsciously—and this is the danger—stall in an excessive need for affirmation. The dynamics of such an unconscious need often run in two directions. The priest can always be affirming himself, verging on bragging, and the people will wonder why he is always talking about himself. Or the priest can manipulate almost everyone he encounters into complimenting and affirming him in his ministry, and then the people often wonder who is ministering to whom. Of course we all need affirmation and must learn to trust and recognize how God intends for us to receive it in the midst of our ministry. When the need for affirmation becomes excessive and unconscious, however, it will forestall the priest's pastoral charity, stripping it of much genuine witness to Christ. The one who is God's faithful, constant affirmation of us all, Jesus, should be the exemplar for the priest in all his daily dealings with people. In this way he fans God's affirming love in Jesus to flame in the midst of the people. Without the requisite religious and human maturity, this charism of availability on the front line misfires and gets stuck in the clutches of the priest's own excessive neediness.

3. Living an Active, Non-monastic Spirituality Founded in a Monasticism of the Heart

This charism has been described in previous parts of this book. Chapter 2 showed that an active, non-monastic spirituality must motivate diocesan priesthood. The most important task in seminary formation is to discover whether or not God is giving a man the gift of active, non-monastic spirituality and whether he is capable of joyously and genuinely living the dynamics of this active-apostolic presence in the world.

Chapter 3 showed how superficial and out of focus such an active spirituality would be without the essential foundation of a monasticism of the heart. The depth of one's solitude and personal experience of Jesus' own utter reliance on God alone must lay a foundation in the seminarian for many years of faithful availability and for pastoral charity over the rest of his life. Serious evidence of a man's inability to integrate active spirituality with a monasticism of the heart would be one sign that this charism is not being given to him and would therefore raise doubts that God is calling him to diocesan priesthood.

4. Not Called to the Commitment of Consecrated Life

Though this is stated negatively, it does set diocesan priesthood off from the ordained priesthood of consecrated Religious Life. Once again, this is an important area to be explored during a program of priestly formation. Too often in the past, elements of the Religious Life commitment have been mistakenly associated with diocesan priesthood. Unrealistic expectations regarding life in community, the practice of gospel simplicity (poverty),[7] and other elements have kept diocesan priests from clearly under-standing and living their own calling in the church. As we will see later in more detail, avoiding the practices of community living and gospel simplicity as they are understood in consecrated Religious Life does not excuse the priest from all experience of these two elements. Discovering and embracing the sense of community and of gospel simplicity appropriate to the diocesan priesthood is another important aspect of seminary formation.

One final caution: A very misleading attitude, often more subliminal than explicit, is still rampant in the church. This is the attitude that diocesan priesthood does not require a seriousness about spirituality similar to that which characterizes monastic and active Religious Life. Certainly diocesan priesthood must be distinguished from these two other vocations in the church; this is precisely the point of this fourth charism in the distinctive spirituality of the diocesan priesthood. But in distinguishing diocesan priesthood from these other two vocations, the intention is not to decrease the spiritual seriousness of diocesan priests. Rather, it is to concentrate the focus of their seriousness on the right point, which concerns the profound spirituality that is distinctive of—and necessary to—their own calling. To strip diocesan priests of serious preparation and concern for spiritual growth, whether the priests do this to themselves or whether others in the church take on this misunderstanding, affects a major part of the church's pastoral ministry.

5. Ordained to Re-present Jesus As Head of the Body

This charism is an important one in the identity of the diocesan priesthood and yet is not easily understood or lived in these days. Through ordination, the priest receives a power, an authority, to make Jesus present in a special way. The priest is able to act *in persona Christi Capitis* (in the person of Christ the Head) and thus to make Jesus present, in the midst of the local people, as head and shepherd. This is not simply the personal gift of an individual priest. This charism involves an office of authority and leadership and has implications far beyond the competency, training, and special giftedness of any individual priest in a parish. This charism of priesthood must always stay in close relationship with the universal priesthood of all believers, yet this power is not simply a carbon copy of the baptismal commitment. The call to ministerial priesthood is a further specification and development of the priestly gift and power that are so foundational as to distinguish the baptized from the unbaptized. This distinctive role of authority and service in the whole Body of Christ first takes its foundation from the radical reorientation of baptism and then springs from a call—not given to all—to the specific development of ministerial priesthood. The power of this office of authority and leadership, though it results from a special call of Jesus, is not automatic in its effectiveness but must be received, assimilated, and—most important—appropriately lived and expressed by a particular priest in the midst of a specific local people.

In an age excessively biased in favor of egalitarianism and against almost anything that rings of authority, the proper assimilation and expression of this power is anything but easy. In *Pastores Dabo Vobis,* John Paul II, after clearly enunciating this authority as part of the identity of the ordained priest, immediately speaks of the humble servant mentality of Jesus as central to the priest's assimilation of this power to act in the person of Christ the Head. In fact, John Paul II sees the authority and servant mentality as coinciding in Jesus. "The authority of Jesus Christ as head coincides then with his total, humble, and loving dedication on behalf of the church."[8] In our contemporary cultural context, however, two extremes gnaw at a priest's heart. He may either, in an overly conciliatory spirit, deny the office of authority given or, in a menacing spirit, flash this authority in people's faces. Both extremes defeat the unity of the Body that is intended in the service of this gift of authority. A body without a head wanders confused, at loose ends and without clear direction; a body that is all head is a freakish creature. The quality of mutual relationship between the priest who makes Jesus present as head and the other members of the Body ultimately determines the unity and effectiveness of the Body.

To act appropriately in the person of Christ the Head always involves more than the discrete sparks of specific actions; a whole way of living ignites the flame. Various people in the Body can act in the person of Christ. Parents do it in raising their children. Catechists do it. Without doubt, however, the ordained priest has a power and authority that go beyond these other actions. While ordination confers an ontological power for Christ to act through priests, their acting in some special way in his person will catch fire, first and foremost, from Christ's all-encompassing paschal deed and then from their own integrated living and praying with and in his person. A whole spirituality of entering the mentality and example of Jesus is involved here if a priest is to live and act out this charism in an appropriate way. Therefore, acting in the person of Christ the Head always involves the deeply personal relationship to which Paul invited the Philippians: "In your minds you must be the same as Christ Jesus" (Philippians 2:5).

The priest's proper exercise of this office of authority is always intimately interrelated with the priesthood of all the faithful. Such authority is never meant to be an exercise of raw power, autocratically imposed without careful concern for the mature development, unity, and mission of the local people. No, the office and authority of ministerial priesthood are essentially oriented to the unity and the mature practice of the baptismal priesthood of all the faithful. Vatican II, in *Lumen Gentium,* the Dogmatic Constitution on the Church, claims that these two priesthoods, though they differ in essence and not simply in degree of importance, nonetheless are carefully interrelated.[9]

To act in the person of Christ the Head does not lift the priest above or separate him from the parochial community. Just the opposite. The people flourish on the inspiration that comes from the priest, and he likewise flourishes on the inspiration from his people. Cardinal Mahony, in a recent pastoral letter on ministry, points out that "in headship, the ordained minister is in the Church, not above the Church, or apart from the Church."[10] The cardinal stresses the need for a truly collaborative, inclusive ministry of the ordained and the nonordained in the Body of Christ. In another part of his letter he says, "True collaboration requires an appreciation of the distinction and differentiation of roles and responsibilities in the body of Christ, together with a clear recognition of the fundamental equality of all the baptized, ordained and nonordained."[11] For this reason he claims that when the priest appropriately acts in the person of Christ the Head, he is a sign of "ecclesial communion."[12] This charism, while conferring genuine authority, essentially relates the priest to the Body of Christ.

For this charism to be effective, the heart of the priest must burn with the same fire that even now inflames the heart of the Risen Jesus in sacrificial self-giving. As this is already happening in the Risen Jesus, so it must become increasingly the case for the priest and for all believers This love dramatically shines from a cross on Calvary, where even in the chaotic darkness an eternal flame glows to the end of the universe—and beyond. Without such an enlivened spirituality, this charism and office of authority become hollow and susceptible to formalistic maneuvering, which surely defeats its purpose.

6. A Lifestyle Distinctively Marked by the Three Evangelical Imperatives of Chastity, Obedience, and Poverty

These three virtues are centrally evangelical. They cut to the heart of Jesus' person and witness and resound imperatively in the hearts of all serious disciples of Jesus. As part of the distinctive spirituality of diocesan priesthood, they play a unique role in the life and ministry of the priest and, as qualities of soul, carve a profound image on the priest's identity. These central virtues are not a part-time venture, nor are they restricted to the superficial dimension of external actions to be performed. Each of the three virtues roots the priest's identity in God's love alone, described in chapter 3 as a monasticism of the heart. Each invites—and gives expression to—that reliance on God alone that Jesus knew throughout his life and that had its highest expression in his Calvary abandonment to the Beloved of his heart. These imperatives promise a similar intimacy, a fire of loving zeal that is known only in such a full-hearted abandonment. Since these three evangelical imperatives are centrally important to the identity and lifestyle of the diocesan priest, I will return to them in the last three chapters of this book.

7. A Spousal Relationship

In the Latin Rite of the Catholic Church at this time, the diocesan priest's commitment involves a promise of celibate chastity. This promise marks the priest with a spousal mentality and relationship. In a culture still rife with self-protective individualism and fear of making permanent commitments, a spousal relationship is not easily understood and appreciated nor much admired. The beauty of self-gift and loving abandonment between bride and bridegroom can seem unreal or old-fashioned, and perhaps not even possible. In the intimacy of spousal love and relationship, the sharing between bride and bridegroom has many aspects: sexual, genital, psychological, spiritual, economic, and many more. Our weak, limited human condition cannot tame the foundational yearning of the human heart for *all*. Thus spouses, who at times tremble in fear of their weakness, yearn inherently for a totality in the consecration of their love. Any overt holding back on the part of a spouse ruptures the relationship—causing doubt, fear, second-guessing, withdrawal. It would be a mistake, and one our oversexed culture is easily capable of, to limit spousal love to the beauty and passion of the genital aspect.

It is also a mistake to limit spousal love to the experience of marriage. In the long Christian tradition, baptism submerges a person in that eternal spring of spousal love that flows freely and clearly at the heart of human relationship with God in Jesus. The Incarnation and the great paschal victory of God in Jesus on Calvary reestablish that original covenant of intimate spousal love for every human being. "Like a young man marrying a virgin, so will the one who built you wed you, and as the bridegroom rejoices in his bride, so will your God rejoice in you" (Isaiah 62:5). Jesus' spousal love and fidelity are at the core of baptismal Christian faith. This spousal love and fidelity quicken a whole relationship initiated and invited by Jesus himself, one that promises an intimacy that will expand right into eternity. The daily life of faith for every Christian believer is a response to such spousal love and relationship. Though this spousal image can be off-putting for some men, the reality of such an interpersonal relationship with God in Jesus—for both the married and celibate—should not be overlooked.

In a way unique to himself, the celibate priest shares this intimate spousal love of Jesus for the church. Because of his vocation and ordination, he is granted a special power to present Jesus Christ as head and shepherd of the whole body. As a result, the celibate priest, standing alone without marital mate, can witness to this spousal love of Jesus for the church in a symbolism and style different from, but not superior to, the witness of married spouses.

This spousal mentality and witness of the diocesan priest also inspires his ministry in the midst of a local people. Beyond witnessing in a special way to the unique spousal relationship with Jesus, the priest, says John Paul II, "is called to be the living image of Jesus Christ, the spouse of the church."[13] Though always a brother believer alongside his other brothers and sisters in the community, the priest, by virtue of his configuration to Christ as head and shepherd, "stands in this spousal relationship with regard to the community."[14] As John Paul II continues, he concretizes the daily witness of this spousal love for the church.

> In his spiritual life, therefore, he is called to live out Christ's spousal love toward the church, his bride. Therefore, the priest's life ought to radiate this spousal character, which demands that he be a witness to Christ's spousal love and thus be capable of loving people with a heart which is new, generous and pure, with genuine self-detachment, with full, constant and faithful dedication and at the same time with a kind of 'divine jealousy' (cf. 2 Corinthians 11:2), and even with a kind of maternal tenderness capable of bearing the 'pangs of birth' until 'Christ be formed' in the faithful (cf. Galatians 4:19).[15]

So the celibate priest witnesses in a distinctive way to Jesus' spousal love, first for every believer and then for the whole body of the church. Whether or not it is appropriate to speak of "being married" to Jesus and to a local diocesan people can be a matter of individual taste and preference. Nonetheless, as part of his identity, the priest experiences a loving commitment to and faithful responsibility for his people that is similar to the love and care of a spouse for the family. The rich intimacy of personal religious experience involved in the celibacy of diocesan priesthood should not be denied. The fire of spousal love flaming at the heart of each individual believer and at the heart of the unity of the whole body needs to be symbolized, facilitated, and cared for. This is part of the role of the celibate priest as soul doctor and guide into the white-hot center of that mysterious fire. It is hoped that a personal dislike of the spousal image on the part of any priest will not distract him from celibacy's invitation to a profoundly personal, intimate relationship with Jesus and with a local diocesan people.

Chapter 11, on diocesan priestly celibacy, will provide further background and enrichment for the spousal relationship introduced here.

8. "Territorial" with a Special Relationship to the Ordinary

The first two charisms of this chapter described the diocesan priest as an ordinary priest always available on the front line in the midst of ordinary people. In this eighth charism a limited territoriality is seen as part of the definition of diocesan priesthood. This insight was not easy, at first, for me to grasp. It seemed that being limited to one particular diocese would somehow curtail a priest's availability and generosity. However, I have come to appreciate how essential—and how beautiful—the relationship between the diocesan priest and his local people is. To be called from and prepared to serve the people in the territory of a particular diocese is not any less generous or challenging than the Jesuit vision of serving the greater glory of God through universal availability. In fact, beyond any detrimental sense of comparison or superiority, service within a limited territory can be precisely the appropriate concrete expression for a diocesan priest of the universal availability of his heart in service of God's greater glory.

The diocesan priest is centered in a specific diocese and at home with a particular parochial people. An availability for any and all dioceses is not, and should not be expected to be, the ideal for the diocesan priest. At times, special missionary needs invite a readiness to serve beyond the boundaries of a priest's diocese or even of his country, but these are always exceptions. The heart of the diocesan priest always longs to be serving in the midst of a parochial people. While it is right and proper that the diocesan priest's vision of ministry is ordinarily focused in a particular diocese, his availability there must keep him ready for a wide variety of parochial and other diocesan ministries.

Since it is part of the basic definition of a diocesan priest, a limited territorial ministry does not in itself compromise his generosity, but certain pitfalls must be avoided. The limited territoriality can unknowingly slide into a limited generosity of heart. When this happens, a priest's availability in a parish becomes part-time, halfhearted, and too limited. He may work only with youth or the elderly and never lead certain devotional practices among the people, for example. Though in the reality of life we all have gifts and preferences as well as deficiencies regarding specific parochial ministries, any unduly limited presbyteral availability curtails the ministerial effectiveness of the whole parish and of the diocese. Another danger to be avoided is the fizzling of a legitimate territorial limitation into an excessively narrow parochial mentality. The diocesan priest must never be anything less than a priest of the whole church and of a whole diocese. The limited territorial focus of the priest's ministry, therefore, must not slake the fire of a full-hearted generosity.

This essential territorial dimension of diocesan priesthood is rooted in the priest's special relationship with the ordinary of the diocese. In Vatican II's decree on the ministry and life of priests, this mutual relationship is highlighted. It speaks of the bishop's "heavy responsibility for the sanctity of his priests" and of priests' standing "by their bishop in sincere charity and obedience."[16] Recently, Bishop Matthew Clark of Rochester, New York, stressed the mutuality of the relationship.[17] Priests have an important role to play in the sanctification of their bishop. As Vatican II puts it, "the bishop should regard priests as his brothers and friends."[18]

Radiating from this special relationship with his bishop is the opportunity for a priest to put a personal face and presence on the institutional and hierarchical dimensions of the church, which often seem very distant and coldly impersonal to people. Walter Burghardt, S.J., states bluntly the challenge of this opportunity: "The point is, the priest does represent an institution. No matter how charismatic, how prophetic, even if called to protest the sins and corruption of institutions, of the church itself, the priest must represent more than his personal insights."[19] A bishop who is liked and admired by all makes the priest's task of representing him a quite different undertaking than that of representing a bishop who, for whatever reasons, is feared and disliked. In developing this aspect of the priest's relationship with his Ordinary, I do not mean to blame anyone or to lay sole responsibility at the feet of the bishop. This relationship of bishop and priest is central to a diocese and its ministerial effectiveness, and the critical need for this relationship to be mutual cannot be stressed enough.

Finally, the heart of this charism invites the priest to a genuine at-homeness in the midst of the local people. To be at home among the people, to be gratefully welcomed by them, and neither to deny nor to exaggerate his special relationship with the bishop—such a special presence among the people will involve for the priest a large dose of being at home with himself. Without such a sense of peace and self-acceptance, a priest will unwittingly be misled into ploys of either inferiority or superiority to the people—rather than displaying a genuine graced sense as brother to them all in Christ.

CHAPTER 5

The Priest As a Leader of Prayer

This chapter will group together six charisms that relate to a priest's ability and readiness to lead the prayer of his local people. As an ordained priest, he is—and must be—a leader of prayer in a great variety of situations. The charisms gathered here describe the priest's involvement with word and worship as two basic fonts of his holiness.

1. Facilitating the Prayer Experience of the People

To pray in any genuine way always involves more than words. Especially in formal vocal prayers, the heart's experience of God's loving presence as foundation for the familiar words makes all the difference. As a leader of prayer in the midst of the people, the priest's sharing of his own experience of God's loving presence can facilitate the people's response to the Holy Spirit's inspiration for their own prayer. The life of the priest, simply because of who he is, is often crowded with saying sacred words and doing holy actions, whether in an overtly religious setting or in a public, secular one. These frequent invitations to public prayer challenge the priest's heart to deepen his reflective faith relationship with God in the fire of the Holy Spirit.

The challenge related to prayer leadership within a parochial community has many different aspects. First, rather than simply mouthing the words, the priest must learn to get his heart into the variety of prayers presented in the ritual. Simply reciting these vocal prayers of the church escapes the challenge of faith. After countless experiences with these formal prayers, how does he keep these prayers alive with the fire of his own religious experience? This is surely not automatic, but neither is it impossible. The extent to which the innate power of these prayers comes alive will depend on how prayerful and sensitive his heart is as he comes to the human situation God desires to bless through this specified vocal prayer.

The priest must also learn to pray spontaneously in a way appropriate to the situation. This is not a gift that comes simply with the laying on of hands; it is a grace to be received in experience over time. Unashamedly and unaffectedly to put the prayer of one's heart into words has its own power in the Holy Spirit to touch other hearts. A priest who is still struggling to exercise the charism of prayer leadership will continue to reflect on the times when his spontaneous prayer was really just him "showing off," as well as those times when his rote use of the ritual was a result of his cowardice in the face of an invitation to pray spontaneously.

The priest's own understanding and experience of prayer are crucial to the exercise of this charism. In a noisy, distracted public scene, quickly to mouth the words of grace before a meal can have a very different effect than that of a briefly explained silence inviting people to touch the fire in their own hearts, followed by a spontaneous prayer carefully fitted to the people in this situation. The quality of the priest's own faith life will determine his readiness in these various encounters. The easier, but often less inspiring way is simply to mouth the given words.

A variety of responses are possible in the many occasions when a priest is asked to pray publicly. Whether he is asked to say grace before a meal, bless a rosary, request health for the sick, or pray in countless other ways, the quality of his own faith and prayer experience will determine his response. At the heart of prayer are an immediacy and a directness of address that are sometimes, but not always, beyond words. There is quite a difference among the following "prayers": first, "Let us pray that God will bless this food . . ."; second, "We ask God to bless this food . . ."; and third, "God of great kindness and care for us all, please bless and nourish us as we share this food." This final example is addressed directly to God and is genuine personal prayer from a heart alive in God's goodness and faithful presence in Jesus. It has an immediacy, a fire, that the first two do not have.

I do not want to be misunderstood here. Priests must learn to pray with an immediacy of religious experience both in the vocal prayer of the ritual and in the spontaneous prayer of their hearts. I am not suggesting that one of these is always better. I am also very aware that spontaneous prayer for each individual priest must be unself-conscious and in his own style as inspired by the Holy Spirit. I have presented a number of specific aspects here in order to flesh out the concept of the priest as leader of prayer in the midst of the people. This is not some easy office of prestige. Without a spiritual identity profoundly rooted in the experience of God's faithful, loving call, the priest will not be ready to quicken the fire of the people's prayer into flame. He will give in to the temptation that every priest knows—to pray in the easier, less heartfelt way. Finally, this profound identity in God's love hearkens back to the monasticism of the heart that can help the priest to avoid the danger Karl Rahner called the "manufacturer of ritual" syndrome.[1]

2. Dramatizing His Own Religious Experience While Exercising the Inherent Power of the Sacraments

Liturgy is always a dramatic action in which the power of God's saving love is primarily operative through the mediation of human ministers. The priest plays a dramatic role in the administration of each of the sacraments for which he is minister. This dramatic element is an art, a gift from God that must be received, learned, and expressed. By dramatizing his own religious experience, the priest invites the people to gather their religious experience for the unified, integrated reception and celebration of God's saving love here and now. It is easy to imagine a priest "staging" his experience in a way that could shock, frighten, astound, or actually displace the people in their experience. These showy ministrations always interfere with the full experience of the sacrament.

Any self-dramatization of the priest is out of place and can distract from, if not conceal, the essential action of Christ in the sacrament. However, the very nature of a sacrament invites, even begs for, appropriate human dramatization in order to represent the action of Christ. The priest's dramatization is not of self but of the flame of holiness in God's deeply personal love always radiant in the presence of the Risen Jesus, which invites special glowing expression in the sacramental encounter of the here and now. Sacraments do not administer themselves. A priest meekly unsure of himself and just "standing by" or one rushing through the rite can each just as easily interfere with the full reception of the sacramental grace offered to the people as does the priest who overplays his role. Though many elements will influence the priest's dramatic staging—the different meanings and the inter-relationship of the sacraments, the geographical setting, the size and type of community—nonetheless, his dramatic role is key to the Body's celebration. Acting in the person of Christ the Head, the priest is inviting and focusing the Body for this special experi-ence of God's love, still radiant in Jesus for the saving unity of all.

3. Regularly Praying the Liturgy of the Hours . . . and Beyond

The Liturgy of the Hours is a special prayer book for the priest. He promises at his diaconate ordination to pray for the people of God in the praise and thanksgiving of the various Hours, united with Jesus before the throne of a God whose love gives life to us all. In this prayer the priest's mentality is crucial. Once again, simply to mumble the words is the easy temptation, but such a heartless exercise will not endure. Rather, the priest is invited to enter the chorus of praise and thanksgiving that rises to God from all of creation, to share in that chorus of prayer and to focus it for the people. Therefore, he never prays this liturgy alone. Though his brother priests are not physically present as they are in the monastic communitarian lifestyle, the priest must mentally reach out in union to them and to the whole people. Without this communitarian atti-tude, the prayer is stripped of its basic power and significance.

An important challenge of seminary formation is to help the future priest discover the Liturgy of the Hours as a prayer book and not just a book of random prayers to be said. An important part of the transition from the seminary experience of praying these Hours with each other to the frequent occasions of praying them alone as a priest is the formation of the appropriate communitarian attitude, whereby the priest never prays this liturgy alone. Just to reach for the book is to renew a mentality that should have developed over years of formation and so is now readily available to him.

To enter the spirituality of the Liturgy of the Hours is to be with the Risen Jesus in his constant praise and thanksgiving with all creation before his Beloved. This stance of prayer invites the priest to remain discerningly aware of his own daily experience and thus to find much for which he desires to praise and thank God. Though the Liturgy of the Hours serves a different purpose in a monastic lifestyle, as we saw in chapter 2, it has its own special way of making prayerful the busy life of the priest—but only if it is prayed with a fidelity and flexibility appropriate to his active life of ministry. In praying the daily Liturgy of the Hours, the priest who lives, prays, and acts in the person of Christ the Head is now, in some related way, also praying in the name of the church (*in persona ecclesiae*) as he intercedes for the people.

Gisbert Greshake, in his book *The Meaning of Christian Priesthood,* says that

> if anyone thought that this [i.e., the prayer of the Liturgy of the Hours] was enough, he would be quite mistaken. Important as the prayer of the Breviary is, it "lives" by the fact that it is founded on personal prayer. Without long, persevering and personal prayer, the fixed form stiffens into an empty, dead formality, which ultimately one goes through and gets finished with, or to which one turns only "when one feels like it."[2]

This states the case loud and clear for another type of personal prayer in the life of the priest, beyond the Liturgy of the Hours and the Eucharist. A prayer of the heart, in solitude, alone with God—often beyond words—plumbs a depth in the priest's heart and in his identity with Jesus.

Though it may often focus on the scriptural reading of the day, this prayerful encounter is more a matter of *being with* than of doing and saying. To enter the room of his own heart, to step somehow behind his public persona, to be alone with God, to encounter that fire of love flaming in the heart of Jesus the High Priest is an experience that scours, purifies, calms, and renews the focus of the priest's identity and ministry. This daily time of prayer in solitude keeps the priest in touch with the monasticism of the heart discussed at some length in chapter 3.

In this type of prayer the priest meets God at a depth and in a quiet intimacy not usually possible in the Eucharist or the Liturgy of the Hours, important as they also are for his life. Though his active ministry will keep the time and length of such prayer flexible, to barter it away in the rush of each day will have disastrous effects on the priest's ministry. In active-apostolic spirituality, this kind of solitary prayer has an enormous ministerial importance. In my opinion, many diocesan priests see this type of prayer as essential to consecrated Religious Life but not to their own spirituality. I think an important change regarding this matter must occur in seminary formation, in the transition into the early years of priesthood, and in the mature ministry of priests. This praying alone with God has its unique way of tending the white-hot heat of God's love at the priest's core and of fanning the flame of desire for serving that love among the people. It is in this solitude with a beloved God that the priest finds a fire to inflame everything in his day and then discovers in the actual enactment of his tasks sparks of promise and hope.

To pray regularly the Liturgy of the Hours and the prayer of solitude creates a daily life of prayer for the priest that does not segregate him from ministry but rather inflames his ministry with the fire of love that Jesus knew in his own life and ministry. The busy priest will find that just as the Liturgy of the Hours and this solitary prayer enrich one another, so will his prayer and ministry have an interrelationship that is key to the enriching integration of the active-apostolic dynamic into his life and work. Oftentimes, in an apparently ordinary fashion, a loving God is being found in a busy life. In reality, this is anything but ordinary; a fire of love, incapable of extinction, is burning a zealous gratitude into a busy heart.

4. Praying, Living, and Preaching the Word with Authority

Though the ministry of preaching is not unique to the ordained priest, it is a central part of his ministry among the people. Whether or not this gift is given must be seriously explored in seminary formation, where quality homiletic training will develop the future priest's best use of this gift. Preaching the word is another way that the priest regularly makes Jesus present as head and shepherd of the people.

Preaching is more than clear enunciation in a well-modulated voice. It is more than reading someone else's published homily. Inspired preaching involves more than staying in touch with the latest TV sitcoms, with stories in the local paper, and with the parish bulletin-board announcements of the events of the week. True preaching focuses, with an inspirational ring of authority, on the fire of God's love in Jesus and springs from the priest's whole experience of living, praying, and acting in the person of Christ in the midst of this parochial people. In this way a homily is born in the Holy Spirit through the priest's contemplation of the word of the readings and through his awareness of the present situation of his people. Preaching and sharing brief daily reflections invites the priest into a profound familiarity—a becoming whom he contemplates[3]—both with Jesus as the Word of God and with his people in their needs. Avery Dulles, S.J., commenting on the priest's ministry of the word, says: "The word that he speaks as priest is not just a word about God, such as the theologian might utter. The priest as witness finds himself possessed by the word of which he is the bearer. The word, spoken rightly, wants to absorb the whole life of the priest and subject it to itself."[4]

Preaching of this type will have an authority that rings with the inspiration of the Holy Spirit, a ring not diverted by authoritarian threats. Preaching with the true ring of the Holy Spirit informs the minds and inflames the hearts of the listeners—and of the preacher. If the priest is not preaching as much to himself as to the gathered congregation, the word, treated too much as his own, will be overly didactic or even self-righteous.

I have two concluding comments about this charism. Reading the word of God is different from any other reading. This reverent, holy reading must be learned, especially in our rapid communication culture in which reading is often rushed or completely bypassed. The priest himself must learn this special reading and help lectors to learn it. This reading waters the dry ground of yearning hearts and cannot be rushed. Finally, holy and inspired preaching demands a deep respect and love for the word as nourished in regular prayer in solitude. Only such prayerful time, only such being alone in and with Jesus, aflame with love for us all, only such standing, kneeling, and sitting in the fire can ignite the "fire in the belly"[5] needed for effective preaching. The renowned preacher Walter Burghardt, S.J., reminds us that "save possibly for a consummate actor, pulpit passion, fire in the belly, is not an emotion a preacher can fake, manufacture at will."[6] Therefore, to preach the word in the person of Christ as a gifted part of his call invites the priest into that fire, based in a profound spirituality whereby his preaching can ring with the love of Jesus the High Priest and not just with the shrillness of his own voice.

5. Preserving a Healthy Sense of Personal Sinfulness

Every serious Christian disciple knows a newness of life that radiates from Jesus himself—God's forgiveness for us all. This forgiving love has an ongoing transforming effect in our hearts, and as a result we must also radiate that forgiveness for others. Jesus makes it very clear that we cannot stop short of forgiving even our enemies. This forgiveness, the very identity of Jesus, is meant not only to transform each of our own hearts but also to heal and reconcile all of our relationships, extending through the whole universe. Serving in the midst of a local people, the diocesan priest is a special sacramental minister making present this transforming forgiveness of Jesus.

This special ministry springs from a divine power conferred in ordination that must then be enfleshed in a priest's daily life of forgiveness. The power to forgive sins belongs to God. Jesus was reminded of this by the scribes in Capernaum. "Who can forgive sins but God?" (Mark 2:7). To exercise this divine power, more is needed than a careful knowledge of the ritual and a comfortable reconciliation room. Receiving the gift of God's forgiveness involves an intricate and intimate set of dynamics for every human person. To be a good forgiver in the name and power of Jesus, the priest must have a reflective, experiential grasp of these dynamics. To minister the forgiveness of God in Jesus is another aspect of the diocesan priest's role as soul doctor and as leader of prayer in the midst of the people. We will investigate this charism much more fully in chapter 10.

6. Maintaining a Theologically Trained Mind and Heart

The priest's prayer leadership of a local people cannot simply be a matter of individual devotion. This type of prayer can become too narrowly focused and inappropriately sentimental. Let me not be misunderstood—personal devotion is an important part of any mature personal relationship with Jesus. People have always found inspiration in the example of Mary and the saints, seen as exemplifying Jesus as God's dream and vision for the whole universe. Thereby, such personal devotions are always rooted in a profound personal relationship of heart with God in Jesus. Without this profound rooting, any particular devotion is superficial, like a reed blowing in the wind, usually broken or uprooted.

For this reason, the priest, as leader of prayer among the people, needs a theologically trained mind and heart. This theological training provides direction and fire for the priest's prayer. The prayerful reflection of theologians over the centuries on God's central revelation of love in Jesus must enlighten, stretch, and shape the priest's intellectual and affective involvement in prayer. The integration of mind and heart is always important in the study of theology. Sometimes an intellectually gifted mind expertly formed in theology can serve as a sword and shield to overwhelm people and keep them at a safe distance, especially if the priest's answers always seem to be articulately at hand and detached from much sensitivity of heart. This charism underlines the importance of serious intellectual, theological formation. A compassionate priest must rely on more than native intelligence stocked with all the answers if he is to appreciate people's questions and always welcome the questing heart with respect and reverence.

This kind of theological formation cannot be completed with ordination, but something would have failed if a theological curiosity had not been lit that could guide a priest's reading and continuing education over the years. This theological cast of mind and heart will not only guide the authentic development of the priest's prayer, preaching, and entire ministry but also will shine like a flame inviting a similar intellectual curiosity and healthy development among the people.

The Priest As Pastoral Leader

In chapters 4, 5, and 6, I am sketching a picture of diocesan priesthood by describing a variety of charisms given by God as signs of a call to this vocation. In chapter 4, I looked at charisms that delineate the nature of this priesthood and its distinctive active spirituality with some focus on its identity. In chapter 5, I concentrated on charisms related to the priest's role as a leader of prayer in the midst of a local people. Now, in this sixth chapter, I will consider the charisms related to the priest's pastoral leadership. It is always dangerous to make too much of a separation between identity and pastoral ministry, and dividing the leadership in prayer from that of pastoral ministry is another ambivalent separation. The significance of these various aspects is quite subtle and therefore involves a lot of overlapping. I remind the reader again that we are concerned with a composite picture, so overlapping enriches the vision, whereas divisions that are too sharp and artificial will throw the picture out of focus.

In chapter 4, I spoke of the pastoral charity of the priest as being much more than what he does. Pastoral charity is a taproot in the deep, rich earth of his identity, and it makes serious demands on his spiritual and human maturity. As we now look into four charisms of priestly pastoral ministry, I am building on all that I said before about pastoral charity as an identifying sign of a diocesan priestly vocation.

1. Radiates a Discerning Presence in the Midst of a Local People

Many people serve as pastoral leaders in a parish setting. Because of the priest's training and the charisms we have been describing, he exercises a unique pastoral leadership in the midst of the local people that comes with being a priest. Many people come to him with concerns somehow relating to the meaning of life and union with God. They want to get closer to God, to pray better, to find and feel God's love more in their daily lives. They want their faith to be more relevant to their workplaces. The desire for spiritual growth gets expressed in a great variety of ways, but in and through all the concerns and requests there flares the burning restlessness of the human heart yearning for more than it now knows. The priest is not meant always to have the answer, and easy, simplistic answers will not do. Rather, as a pastoral leader, the priest must have a reflective understanding of the dynamics of spiritual growth. This does not require an advanced academic degree in spirituality, but it does require serious study and prayerful reflection to acquire an experiential understanding of what St. Ignatius called *discernment of spirits*.

A professional, experiential grasp of the art of discernment will allow the priest to hear the subtext beneath some people's simple inquiries and to respond intelligently to other people's quite direct spiritual questions. He may never formally teach discernment or use some of the classic terminology, but if he does not really understand and is not consciously living a life of discerned intimacy with God in Jesus, he cannot be a light shining in the midst of the people. Through the example of the priest's discerned life, the fire of the Holy Spirit can allure and enkindle far beyond what he may ever intend or realize. In chapter 9, I will develop more fully the significance of this charism.

2. Radiates a Lively Hope and Encouragement in the Face of Sin, Suffering, and Dying

No proof is needed for the thesis that human life always involves suffering, dying, and evil. It is part of human life, and a part that not one of us enjoys. Rather, it often discourages and frustrates us. When this side of human life is shared with a loving spouse or a compassionate and understanding friend, it does not magically transform the situation, but it does make a difference. As available and present in the midst of his people, the priest often has this tough side of life dropped at his door. To visit the elderly of the parish, to enter the tragedy of a young person's sudden death and celebrate the funeral, to listen patiently and do what can be done to correct the malice of injustice in a family, to receive some people's incessant bickering and criticism without getting stained by it—these are all part of the burden of being so available. How understandable that a priest, at times, would want to run and hide! The charism described here also plunges the priest into a profound spirituality.

It is no surprise that suffering, dying, and the evil of sin are brought to the priest. Doctors and therapists have much of the same daily fare in their work, but the approach and expectation are different with the priest, however, just because he is a priest. The doctor and therapist must learn to keep these encounters in perspective and within professional boundaries, or they will quickly be burned and scarred by these flammable encounters. Though the priest's situation is different, he too can quickly become soured and burned out. In self-protection, he can develop a shell that seems almost impenetrable, a style that is professionally slick and impersonal, or a round of funny stories that seem interminable and are often glaringly insensitive. All these tactics can disguise a fear of death and of appropriate intimacy. However understandable such protection, fear, and awkwardness are, they make genuine compassion impossible.

The issue is not that people have no right to bring this rough side of life to the priest. It is a beautiful, though not easy, part of the diocesan priesthood. If a priest were too protected from this aspect of life, it would signify a defeat in his own pastoral presence. In these situations of hardship and suffering, to convey compassionate hope and encouragement—to be a sign that the last word is life, never death—requires that the priest live as faithfully as he can in the depths of the paschal mystery of Jesus' faithful suffering and death into resurrection.

To convey this hope takes more than just words—it takes a vision for daily life and service. Such a vision is never rigidly set in place forever. It must be renewed regularly in prayer before Jesus in his own experience of unfair suffering leading to Calvary—and beyond. It must be renewed in prayerfully honest reflection on our own weakness, cowardice, and failure in the face of such challenge. This vision of unconquerable hope is a grace, promised and won for us all in the victory of God in Jesus. Constitutive of serious discipleship for all believers, it has special implications for the diocesan priest. It is not a grace that is automatically inserted into the heart at ordination. It is a fire, kindled first in the tinder and coals of the priest's own life and then, if tended over years, fanned to radiant flame. Unless a priest has prayerfully faced the mystery of suffering and dying in the light of the cross and been blessed with compassionate grace, he becomes a countersign to the Good News of Jesus. Then he may get stuck, more than he wants, in the awkward babble of words that cover up a lack of heart.

3. Functions Well within a System Prone to Loneliness and Ambition

Loneliness and ambition within the human condition are always inimical to healthy, productive relationships. Among the people gathered for a particular task, a system of expectations can easily take shape. This usually is not the intention of most, if any, of the participants, but the compelling force of such a system can be very strong, to the point of enslaving many in the group. This phenomenon can happen in all sorts of groups: families, workplaces, political districts, religious congregations, diocesan presbyterates.

Loneliness and ambition are part of the human condition. Their presence and pollution choke all our hearts; their dynamics desolate us and disintegrate the bonding of any group. Both of these inner experiences are self-focused rather than focused on service of God and of other people. They have wreaked havoc in many groups, especially when their dynamics are not honestly detected and confronted.

The diocesan priesthood has its own proneness to loneliness and ambition, which can easily coagulate into a system with harmful effects for the presbyterate and the whole diocese. Unhealthy dynamics riddling a presbyterate always interfere with the service of the people in the diocese. In this charism a priest receives the gift of serving well by developing dynamics counter to the two destructive ones mentioned here. The utter uniqueness of every human person, such a gift and blessing in itself, also creates the potential for a suffocating loneliness. The celibate lifestyle endorses this potential with its own signature, something I will comment on further in chapter 11. My point here picks up an issue mentioned earlier. Without an appropriate communitarian air in the presbyterate, loneliness can so clutch the breathing of a priest and shorten his wind that his ministry suffers.

The communitarian sense appropriate to a presbyterate of busy, gifted priests is not monastic but actively apostolic. Thus, as we described it in chapter 2[1], this sense of community among the priests, while not utterly oblivious to physical presence, at times does not depend primarily on the priests' regular presence to each other. But an attitude—I mean a real mentality, cultivated and developed over years—of being available and serving together in focus around their bishop-brother can make a real difference in priests' hearts, especially when they are living and serving alone.

To feel and to be genuinely treated as part of a larger venture does not remove all experience of loneliness, but it does provide something to grab hold of in prayerful awareness when the waters of loneliness lap, or crash, against the priest's affectivity. Without this communitarian sense, a priest not only feels as if, but *is* all by himself, without what should be a strong life-support system in the suffocating experience of loneliness. As part of this communitarian sense throughout the whole presbyterate, support groups, friendships with priests and others, and other small groupings also provide much support. This writer does not think, however, that these small groupings are enough by themselves; some priests will always be left out. Also, these smaller groupings lack the overall support and identity that not only help with loneliness but also share the fire for ministry in the whole diocese. In chapter 12, on the obedience of the diocesan priest, I will develop this sense of community as related to ministry much more fully.

Ambition is a second dynamic that has an abrasive effect on all human hearts and is destructive of community and ministry. When ambition has zeal and fire for service as its genuine object, it is a valuable gift, but here I am addressing the inevitable underside of that gift. We all have a desire to be known and to be acknowledged for who we are. This is a God-given gift, implanted in us at creation, but this desire can become a drive that enslaves us and destroys our relationships with others. Sometimes within a particular work group, quite specific expectations get set up, almost like benchmarks. To get trapped in this system is always destructive.

The problem with this enslaving sense of ambition is that the priest's heart is straining to be acknowledged and rewarded for what he has done. A certain amount of this desire is healthy and to be expected. God, who made us in our humanity, knows how much we need to be affirmed, and any system should have healthy, balanced rewards for work well done. In the excessive ambition being addressed here, however, this drive to be acknowledged for what has been done has replaced any deeper identity. Of course, the priest is usually not aware of how far this ambitious hunger has spread or of how famished he really is. The charism of being able to function well in such a situation involves what I described in chapter 3 as the monasticism of the heart.

The priest's identity is in God's love alone, faithful from the first moment of the priest's creation and continuing into the fullness of eternal life. This faithful love of God takes most dramatic expression in Jesus' death for him on the cross. This, beyond anyone or anything else, establishes the priest's identity as one who is loved. No one else's love will ever approach this shining, generous act. Living in the light of this loved identity provides an anchor against the tides of ambition. When seen in the light of Jesus on the cross, to minister as assistant pastor for the rest of one's life is not awkward or strange, but a valuable ministry, an outlet for the gratitude of his heart. The call to be a pastor of a prestigious parish or to be a bishop is just that: a call, rather than the object of ambition. It is an invitation to grateful service from a God whose love illumines and beckons beyond the politics of any human situation. To avoid the strong pull of ambitious expectations in the political interrelationships of a presbyterate requires a profound spirituality and a rooting of the priest's identity in God and in a love whose intimacy and effectiveness are beyond anything of this world. The stakes are very high, however: loneliness and ambition will always interfere with the contagiousness of that love's fire among the people.

4. Provides Administration and Stewardship

Some people are born administrators. They love it and often are good at it. For other people, the administrative side of leadership is real drudgery and is approached reluctantly. Since the diocesan priest is a pastoral leader, administration is an unavoidable part of his ministry. Whether he has an innate love for it or not, he cannot avoid ultimate responsibility for the administration of the parish.

Thus the charism of administration is one sign of his diocesan priestly call. Experiences in his training should help him to learn and appreciate his own administrative style. Since he is not the only administrator, with full and total responsibility, he must facilitate a collaborative style of stewardship in the parish. The collaboration of lay parishioners, who are given genuine responsibility and often have professional experience beyond that of the priest, will ensure proper care for the purely administrative aspect of the parish and leave the priest with time and energy for explicitly spiritual ministry. Though the buck may stop at his desk, this cannot prevent genuine delegation in a collaborative fashion, which will also facilitate a greater overall unity of responsibility and stewardship with the people. Such collaboration will not excuse the priest from any involvement in administration. Some of his time will always be spent in this aspect of care for the parish. Collaboration, however, will prevent a situation in which the major role of the priest becomes that of administrative manager rather than spiritual leader.

Though responsibility for the organizational stewardship and temporal administration of the parish cannot be completely bypassed, the priest is above all a spiritual administrator. In this role he calls forth and integrates among the people the gifts of the Holy Spirit, always plentifully bestowed but often not recognized or properly exercised. In this spiritual ministry, delegation and collaboration are again important aspects. The issue here is not simply building a new edifice, but building the Body of Christ; not simply managing payments and debts, but facilitating and discerning the gifts of the Spirit. Such careful priestly tending of the fire kindles a radiance of holiness among the people and a glow of transformation in the whole diocese.

In these ways administration becomes part of the whole spirituality of the priest and of the parish. Often administration is regarded as a secular, professional part of the operation, and when so reduced it does not assume its own rightful spiritual perspective and motivation. Mark O'Keefe, O.S.B., makes the point carefully:

> For many priests, administration, meetings, finances are simply a distraction—maybe even a hindrance—to their spirituality. I am not suggesting that administration is an essential part of priestly ministry but, if it is part of his life, he must incorporate it into his path of holiness. [2]

To place the whole administrative task in the context of shared stewardship for what God has entrusted to us rather than in that of arrogant ownership is to practice a spirituality that is not always easy or fun, but it does preserve the focus of administration and the context within which the priest can find its ultimate meaning. To practice genuine delegation with clear accountability requires a real spirit of trust. When the unpleasant details of administration become overwhelming, gritting one's teeth and charging ahead will usually not be as effective as prayerfully viewing this disliked dimension as one's share, with others, in the paschal mystery of Jesus still at work in the transformation of our world. This renewal of vision will often stimulate the wisdom and courage needed for making the hard decisions.

Conclusion

In summary, these last three chapters have described in some detail the charisms of teaching, preaching, catechizing, and evangelizing, charisms essential to the diocesan type of priest-hood. Above all, as has already been acknowledged, the priest's presence and role of service bring together the gifts of all his people so that they can ponder the word in sacramental communion. These three chapters on charisms make it clear that diocesan priesthood is a distinctive life of active-apostolic spirituality in which the mission of an official position and authority must be integrated with a holiness of personal life. This theme has been integral to this part of the book. Without the fire of the Holy Spirit glowing in the priest's heart and quickening the flame of love, the office of authority will cause the priest to harden into a shell of steely insensitivity to the unity of the people.

In the next two chapters I will show the crucial role these charisms play in the whole process of diocesan priestly formation.

Gold Purified in the Fire: Diocesan Seminary Formation

What Diocesan Priesthood Looks Like

In the next two chapters I will look at some of the implications for diocesan seminary formation in what this book has already presented. The charisms of diocesan priesthood play a central role in seminary formation.[1] If neither seminarians nor staff really know what diocesan priesthood looks like, they will approach the formation process with confusion. If they do not really believe in a distinctive diocesan priestly spirituality, a number of things can happen. A high-powered academic program can assume such a priority that it can enervate, if not replace, a seriousness about spirituality. A spirit of mundaneness can infiltrate a seminary and cause a type of free-floating depression. Nothing is special, there is no challenge, and a disorienting sense of boredom hangs in the corridors. Such a place lacks fire and is not ablaze with the flame of God's love radiating in the heart and on the face of Jesus the High Priest. In such a program, no fire enkindles the hearts of seminarians for future ministry. This absence of fire and missionary motivation produces, at times, a spirit of immaturity and a web of childish relationships. Sometimes, men just leave.

Please do not misunderstand—I am not suggesting a process in which fireworks dramatically explode day after day. Men would burn out early in such a process and would be seriously misled. Human life and spiritual living always involve large doses of the mundane. Awareness of a distinctive diocesan priestly spirituality will not erase this basic ordinariness from life. In fact, maintaining vision and enthusiasm over the long haul of many ordinary times should be one of the chief challenges and tests in any ministry training program. If life always seems exciting and breathless, something unrealistic is being fostered and a basic persevering fortitude can hardly be forged. Awareness of and admiration for what diocesan priesthood and its distinctive spirituality look like will not remove the ordinary from life, but they will provide an ultimate orientation flammable enough to spark both excitement and profundity of motivation.

I speak here of knowing what diocesan priesthood looks like. I am not referring to some eternal, unchanging essence that can be perfectly articulated. If only it were that easy! But two dangers must be avoided. First, in these times of decreasing numbers and growing morale problems, there can be a reactive, ultimately shortsighted tendency to state apodictically, clearly, and fully exactly what diocesan priesthood is. A second tendency is to let diocesan priesthood seem ordinary and quite unspecified so that it is not clear exactly what we are talking about or looking for in a seminary program. Neither of these tendencies ultimately reveals the attractiveness of the diocesan priesthood or serves the people of a diocese well. We must find a balance between these two tendencies. A call to diocesan priesthood is not something quickly and scientifically verifiable. Neither is it something so mysterious that it cannot really be described with much specificity, leaving its identity simply to be intuited. In a true vocational call from God, the mysterious realm of communication and interrelationship between the divine and the human is involved, but many specific characteristics and gifts, called *charisms* in this book, can be identified as constituting diocesan priesthood. The previous three chapters have delineated this territory.

Something More Needed

Vatican II and the new Code of Canon Law view diocesan priestly spirituality in a very different way than did the Council of Trent and the code of 1917.[2] Since Vatican II, there has been much experimentation regarding the program of priestly formation. We have varied the locale (in the country or the city), the course of study, the daily schedule, and many other things. We have learned a lot from this experimentation, and seminary programs across this country reveal a widespread diversification as a result.

Finally, however, as this book has tried to make clear, something more than the superficial, though not unimportant, elements of locale and schedule is at issue in contemporary seminary formation. No quick, simple solution exists for the basic challenge facing diocesan priestly life and ministry today. No new set of pastoral skills or administrative strategy will suffice. The issue cuts deeper than any priestly image of speech, activity, or clothing, though these concerns have their own relative importance. No, the crisis here calls us into the core issues of spiritual identity. The attempt to make a number of necessary adaptations of superficial aspects without reviewing the core of diocesan priestly identity and formation is doomed, in the long run, to failure. Our concern must plumb the depths of the matter.

A Matter of Identity in God

Only an identity profoundly rooted in God and stirred in response to a love beyond all imagining can assure faithful, zestful service in a diocesan priestly vocation, something far more attractive and compelling than sheer survival. The reality of God's love as revealed and proclaimed in Jesus, while sounding the depths of the priest's identity, also induces a relationship with the church in a presence and availability to God's people. A priestly heart cannot simply be stretched further and further to achieve the freedom and flexibility expected today for the great diversity of priestly tasks. This requisite availability and mobility can never be accomplished simply through the addition of new teachable skills and techniques or the realignment of old ones. We are not speaking here of the heart as though it were a rubber band always capable of stretching further without snapping. No, the image and the approach we are discussing are very different.

GEORGE A. ASCHENBRENNER, S.J.

We are speaking, rather, of such a profoundly personal experience of God's love, as core identity, that a priest is then able to radiate this love with a surprising diversity and availability in daily ministry. The extraordinary diversity of service and availability required of diocesan priests is a serious invitation to an ever-deepening identity rooted in God's love alone. We cannot be inattentive to this invitation, except at great peril to us all. This identity in God's love alone, more than our own stressful efforts, will stretch our hearts beyond their imagined limits. As a center of identity, such love stretches far beyond anything in this whole universe. This is the identifying, ongoing experience I call the monasticism of the heart.

Priestly Spiritual Formation: Radical Reorientation

If seminary formation is to run deep enough to lay the foundations for a lifelong identity, then radical reorientation of a man, down to the roots of his person and faith, must be involved. In this radical realignment the gamut of a man's motivation is carefully examined: his natural likes and dislikes, his affective sensuality, his hopes, dreams, fantasies, and so much more. This radical scrutiny is not instigated by unwarranted suspicion or doubt of the man's priestly vocation. Quite the contrary! In the next chapter I will describe a presumption for perseverance that should be in operation from the day a seminarian enters a formation program. The concern in this radical realignment is with honest self-knowledge and the confirming experience for the seminarian of finding his own unique identity in Christ, an identity that has been crystallized, revealed, and matured in the charisms of diocesan priestly identity. This is never an easy or obvious discovery.

As difficult and as trying as such formation is meant to be, its purpose is invaluable. Gold is being tested and purified. Without the white heat of fire, the gold will not be refined or revealed in all its radiance. In this time of scarce vocations, we must avoid any false kindness that would soften the challenge of priestly formation by making a program easier than it should be. It is my opinion that the more we acknowledge the radically spiritual challenge and identity of diocesan priesthood, the more attractive such a life of service will be in the church today.

This radical reorientation at the heart of seminary formation is intended to be a formidable challenge for the candidate as well as for the seminary staff. Regardless of a man's age and the background of experience with which he enters the priestly preparation program, he will leave a very different person. The challenge of radical reorientation for the young entrant is quite different from the challenge for the older one, but it is no less incisive. Renewed and realigned in some fundamental ways, with a new identity forged in clarity and precision, the seminarian is much more humbly confident of God's call to this unique priestly service in the church.

If this confidence and clarity are to come, the seminary experience I speak of must involve a type of blood transfusion. Having breathed in the smog and fumes of the radically secular and often unchristian values of contemporary culture for many years, the candidate, good and sincere in many ways, usually has coursing in his bloodstream, quite beyond his own awareness, a spirit diametrically opposed to authentic Christian ministry. Autonomy, individualism, and therapeutic comfort, for example, must be strained out. This is not as simple as siphoning off the contaminated blood and then pumping in a fresh supply of healthy blood. No, the operation is more subtle, delicate, and trying. Healthy strains of these humanistic values must be preserved as the faith of the seminarian is infused with a mature generosity of abandonment and docility to the Holy Spirit. This transfusion requires more than an overnight hospitalization, and without such purification, priestly service will be ambiguous and misleading.

In some ways, as the contemporary cultural development of postmodernity continues, the operation, besides being delicate and trying, will need to be quite radical. Postmodernity is characterized by a radical fragmentation (nothing holds together anymore), a radical relativism (no basis for truth but what each person thinks), and a radical alienation (there is no story I feel part of). As these strains appear in the bloodstream of candidates, the transfusion procedure will be more radical and extensive than in the past. As we face the

GEORGE A. ASCHENBRENNER, S.J.

reality of younger parishioners who are profoundly affected by this developing postmodernity, we must also face the challenge of preparing seminarians for missionary work among people who are good and sincere but basically uncatechized. In this cultural context pastoral ministry becomes genuine missionary work,[3] and seminaries are preparing men to be sent out as missionaries.

Once again, such a radical reorientation and remaking of a man's habitual pattern of mind and heart is not easy, nor is it all fun. On the other hand, neither should it seem like time wasted or time without any enjoyment. A man's deepest, truest self in Christ is being revealed, purified, and forged with exciting, glorious prospects for the future. All the charisms presented in this book are tested, called forth, and revealed over the years of seminary formation. This is the precise point, ultimately, of the radical transformation: a glorious revelation of the gifts God gives in a call to diocesan priesthood. In the midst of all the heat, gold is beginning to sparkle and shine with incredible radiance.

Role of Solitude

In this treatment of seminary preparation for diocesan priesthood, I single out only one essential element. A regular experience of solitude is key to laying the foundation of diocesan priestly identity and active ministry. In the midst of many necessary elements already alluded to in this book, this experience of extensive solitude—of being utterly alone with God—is crucial. A depth of heart is plumbed here in order to lay a foundation that will stand strong over many years. This time alone with and in God is a type of monastic experience, but not the kind that would lead the seminarian into a monastery. Rather, in this aloneness, the monasticism of the heart develops and shapes a profoundly personal identity in God's love that will be continually needed to fan into flame the same fire of faith and zeal that burned in the heart of Jesus in the midst of his busy daily life.

As mentioned earlier in this book, Henri Nouwen in *The Way of the Heart* speaks of this solitude as a furnace of transformation that is needed if a minister's compulsiveness is to become compassion.[4] Compulsive ministry often gets on people's nerves and does not witness nearly enough to God's love, so a transformation is needed and must be part of seminary training. Obviously, lengthy regular periods of solitude are never easy; we sweat, we squirm, we blister, we burn in such a furnace. However, with enough patience and perseverance, and often at the end of his own controlling capabilities, a future priest learns to rely on a Love faithful beyond all others, as Jesus relied on his Beloved's love at Gethsemane and Calvary. In a heated furnace, the combustion of a spark can flame into a fire in his heart and can light a perduring way into the future.

This habit of daily solitude developed over years of formation lays a foundation in at least two ways for future priestly ministry. First, it provides the framework for a daily experience of contemplative quiet and calm alone with God that will anchor an often stormy and turbulent ministry. Second, such solitude becomes a taproot from which spring the requisite flexibility and mobility for active ministry. Such aloneness gives birth to a confident awareness of intimate companionship, with Jesus lovingly co-laboring in all. The fundamental importance of such solitude and the radical reorientation it entails can hardly be overstressed—without it, effective, dependable priestly ministry is unlikely.

Solitude, Community, and Mission for Leadership

This stress on solitude does not give priority to personal spiritual development over training for missionary community. Philip Murnion rightly cautions against such a tendency in modern seminaries.[5] The challenge, in my opinion, is precisely to integrate the personal with the communal and the ministerial and, in fact, to see how fruitless and individualistic ministry becomes without a profoundly personal foundation laid in, and continuing to develop in, solitude. Henri Nouwen also speaks strongly to this relationship between solitude and community in his book *Clowning in Rome:*

> Solitude is the place where we can reach the profound bond that
> is deeper than the emergency bonds of fear and anger. . . . In

GEORGE A. ASCHENBRENNER, S.J.

solitude we can come to the realization that we are not driven together but brought together. . . . Solitude is very different from a time-out from community life. Solitude is the ground from which community grows. . . . Solitude is the place where our common vocation becomes visible. . . . As long as we see the community as a support system to help us realize our individual ideals, we are more children of our time than children of God.[6]

In the fourth chapter of the same book, Nouwen writes glowingly about the essential relationship of contemplation in solitude to ministry.[7] If we are better able to integrate solitude as a foundation for serving in the missionary community of a diocese, then the choice Murnion poses between a year of spiritual formation and a year of pastoral formation becomes a false choice. Spiritual, pastoral, missionary, and communal formation, as essentially interlinked, could provide a year's special experience crucial to all that seminary preparation intends to achieve.

My description here of seminary formation, along with my treatment of the charisms of diocesan priesthood, makes it clear that the overall issue of seminary is formation for priestly leadership. This means that implicit in the presence of the diocesan priestly charisms is a basic potential for leadership on the part of the seminarian. As Murnion reminds us, "It is as leader, not just as an official, that the priest carries out his ministry."[8] This has important implications for the understanding and practice of the priest's charism of acting in the person of Christ the Head, as we have mentioned earlier[9] and as is manifest in *Pastores Dabo Vobis*.[10]

In summary, diocesan priestly formation focuses on a radical reorientation of the seminarian that reveals whether or not the charisms of diocesan priesthood are given. In the heat of this radical reorientation, it is precisely the gold of these charisms that is purified to revelation and fanned to a steady flame of readiness for priestly love and mission. Seminary formation concludes in a glorious moment of humble awareness of God's call to follow and serve in the special priestly ministry of Jesus, whose presence still consecrates the whole people to a spirited love and holiness.

CHAPTER 8

Presumption for Perseverance and Permanence

Perseverance and permanence have never been easy for human beings, nor for cultures or civilizations.[1] These two conditions always require a commitment deeper and more courageous than that of passing fancy and temporary excitement. Yet the dependability of persevering commitment is the very bedrock of any civilization. History reveals plenty of evidence that a gradual fraying of the bonds of permanency sounds a death knell before a full bursting of such bonds finally buries that culture or civilization. In this chapter I will address the development of readiness for priestly perseverance that must take place during the years of seminary formation. I will highlight an important practice that plays a special role in such readiness for the permanency of priestly commitment.

In many ways, recent years have revealed a fragility, a difficulty, and a lack of trustworthiness in many basic personal commitments. A priest who has been ordained ten or fifteen years becomes bored and is tired of his commitment, so he begins to consider another lifestyle. A young priest falls in love, an experience that is healthy enough and not unexpected, but in the tidal wave of such emotion quickly presumes that he has made a mistake in being ordained and seriously ponders leaving active ministry. These are just two examples of circumstances that have resulted in a rather large number of priests leaving their priestly commitment soon after ordination. Something is awry here. In this chapter I will address only one of the many important aspects that make up this complicated phenomenon. My concern is with the diocesan priesthood, but the issue is profound and extensive enough to have implications for any commitment: that of religious life, married life, or of a dedicated layperson.

What has happened in such situations? How do we explain such predicaments? Did the priest not really understand what he was promising? Is seminary preparation not realistic enough for today's world? Many other questions could be and usually are asked—and are often answered with too facile a certainty. A full understanding is very difficult without careful investigation of specific cases.

I am not attempting any full explanation in this chapter, nor, even more important, am I writing in judgment of men in such complicated and stressful situations. My undertaking is more modest. I will describe the intentional exercise of a specific practice that I am calling a presumption for perseverance and permanence. This concrete exercise occurs in the midst of a whole process of presumption of vocation that delineates and motivates the entire seminary program; it runs from seminary entrance until ordination, growing in seriousness and certainty along the way. After showing the importance of such an exercise as part of the future priest's preparation, I will describe the way this experience also prepares the priest for living a permanent commitment far beyond ordination, even until death.

Permanent Commitment in Contemporary Culture

No mature person expects permanent commitment to be easy, but for various reasons its very possibility seems more questionable today than ever before. We have so canonized individual freedom as a supreme human value that responsibility to commitments is too quickly seen as an interference to our freedom. Growth in our appreciation of the developmental phases of human maturity has made us less sure of our ability to commit ourselves to being present and loving far into the future. Consider, after all, how radically and how often our identity will shift as we grow through these different stages (if we get through them at all!). More and more, people have become skeptical of their responsibility over the long haul and so are afraid to make promises that profess their deepest truth, especially in a way that involves a serious commitment of self over many years. From another perspective, contemporary culture has so enthroned autonomy and self-fulfillment that it is hard to talk about commitments that can perdure beyond intensely self-absorbed feelings and projects. Add to these cultural aspects the contemporary postmodern development described briefly in the previous chapter,[2] and the possibility of permanent commitment seems even more dismal.

These concerns in contemporary culture are surely being discussed and, in my opinion, need much more discussion, especially in terms of a philosophy of life rooted in faith in Jesus. Somewhere in all of this, a deep sense of self has either simply been lost or has become so superficially pliable as to seem almost infinitely changeable. Such belief in the radical changeability of self affects even the possibility of a permanent profession of this "self." In some cases, as in postmodernity, the permanent profession of a self is outright denied; in other cases the denial is more subliminal but no less real. However this mistaken conclusion gets imprinted on us, the result is the same and bodes disaster regarding our future together.

Against the backdrop of such serious issues, this chapter is not meant to prove the possibility of permanent commitment; rather, without being insensitive to these torturous questions, I am presuming the possibility of such permanence. Without negating the serious cultural issues involved, I suspect that the denial of any capability for permanent commitment not only seriously dwarfs the profound dignity of human beings but also foolishly suppresses a sense of steadfast heroism that is badly needed today.

Original Presumption: Judgment of Acceptance into Seminary

The acceptance of someone into seminary preparation for priestly ordination must always be a serious decision based on enough preliminary hard evidence of a call and not just on whim or

arbitrary intuition. A first judgment about the presence of the charisms of diocesan priesthood, which have been described in three previous chapters of this book, forms the decision for acceptance of an applicant. Of course, the mystery of a vocation from God can never be completely reduced to a case of perfectly clear evidence. Though the mystery of a vocation is born and intimated in the clear evidence of certain requisite attitudes, gifts, and genuine desire, such a vocation ultimately transcends scientifically verifiable evidence. For this reason a priestly vocation is never so immediately obvious as to bypass the years of serious preparation needed to clarify, develop, and mature the call.

The presumption for priestly perseverance and permanence begins with entrance into seminary and continues to grow throughout one's life, even until death. The initial presumption that begins seminary preparation is a judgment shared by a number of related parties: the candidate himself, the vocation director, the bishop, and the seminary staff. This beginning presumption that opens the doors of the seminary to the candidate must deepen over time so that a year or more before diaconate ordination it can be formalized in a way to be described later in this chapter. This presumption, which is more and more personally assimilated by the candidate, is finally validated by God through the church at ordination. After the church's validation in ordination, the details of priestly life and ministry are carefully discerned by using this validated presumption as a rudder that provides direction and balance in the swells and squalls of daily service. Though this chapter highlights one specific exercise of this continuing presumption, such an exercise must not be extracted from the context of the whole process.

In using the word *presumption* I run the risk of being misunderstood. *Presumption* can seem as arbitrary as a figment of someone's overactive imagination, as selfish as strong-willed determination, or as misguided as a projection of someone's unrealistic fancy. For this reason I cannot stress enough that what I mean by *presumption* here is a judgment based on the evidence of hard facts honestly observed and interpreted. It is a crystallization of grace, a moment of clarity that formalizes the quality of the candidate's loving

relationship with God in Jesus. As a caution against the misunderstandings just mentioned, the presumption must be tested and reflected upon throughout the whole process of priestly preparation.

From the very beginning of seminary, this graced judgment of presumption invites a practical act of faith in the candidate's priestly vocation, first on the part of the candidate himself, then on the part of his spiritual director, his formation advisor, and the whole seminary staff. Serious selectivity of seminary candidates makes this practical faith both possible and importantly rooted in the known history of the man's vocation. At this early stage of presumption the candidate is not very intensely concerned with permanence in his vocation. Still, certain important dynamics of discernment are called into play. Practical trust in one's vocation at this early stage means seeing God's hand in everything that endears such a life to the candidate, whereas anything, however reasonable, that disquiets the heart about such a life is not viewed as an inspiration from God. Living this initial presumption is really a continuation of the vocational discernment that led the candidate to apply to the seminary in the first place. A candidate's careful living of this early presumption can help him avoid the confusion of falling prey to the emotional fluctuation that is always part of daily life. Such early basic vocational discernment will make these ordinary daily experiences instructive and will reveal the divine initiative, motivation, and perdurance of a priestly vocation.

A Later, More Mature Presumption

Years have passed since the presumption of vocation that brought the candidate to the seminary. These years have not been spent completely in the enclosed world of the seminary; rather, they have involved encounters with many people in leisurely and ministerial situations. Study, prayer, and other sharing with fellow seminarians have anchored his vocation beyond his own experience. His personal relationship with the Risen Jesus has also matured through regular prayer and solitude. Competent spiritual direction has helped the seminarian to read the signs of God's loving Spirit in

the quiet of prayer and in the daily details and encounters of life, both when boringly ordinary and when intensely exciting. Such one-on-one spiritual direction has become the central structure in contemporary religious formation. It tailors the whole process of seminary to each candidate and helps him to adapt to and contribute to the present seminary community. In this way the original presumption has been tested and deepened, or the candidate has already departed.

In the last few years of his training, the candidate becomes capable of a more serious and mature exercise of the presumption of his priestly vocation. The necessity of an intentional expression of this presumption, together with what it importantly produces, is the subject of this chapter. At this time, much more than at entry into the seminary, the candidate is capable of appreciating the permanence of priestly commitment. The development of awareness of, appreciation for, and readiness for permanence will vary from candidate to candidate. Because of this, the timing of this expressed presumption cannot be legislated for everyone, whereas events such as the public profession of faith and request for orders can be scheduled and done together. This private exercise of presumption of God's call to the permanence of priestly commitment is the fruit of such a personally paced process of discernment that it prevents any group expression at some expected time. Though this exercise of presumption for permanence does have a strong corporate bonding dimension to it, as expressed here it must fit the Holy Spirit's unique timetable for each individual.

Carefully Timed

The need for appropriate timing will become clear as we further specify the content of this intentional exercise of presumption. Once again, beyond any sentimentalized wish or boyhood dream of priesthood, the content of the presumption of which I speak here is clear and definite. It is the presumption that God is calling a man to diocesan priestly commitment and ministry for the rest of his life, that God is calling a man to diocesan priestly identity until he dies. Of course the whole identity of diocesan priesthood is included here, but the candidate now clearly and intentionally views the permanence and perpetuity of the commitment. As we will soon see, making such a presumption with genuine intentionality is instructive in some very important ways.

Such a presumption can be intended only after a certain maturation of the candidate's human and spiritual experience. A fundamental human maturity in self-acceptance, self-actualization, and self-transcendence is needed if permanent commitment is to have any hope of perseverance; even more important, we are finally seduced to "forever" by God in an overwhelming experience of the eternal flame of Jesus' faithful love. This experience of this love does not necessarily register for the candidate as a subjectively peak experience, but its objective reality, when believed and assimilated, lures him away from tight, selfish control of his own life. It entices him to an intimate trust whereby he leaves the control and guidance of his life to the God of faithful love promised in Jesus. The permanence and perseverance I speak of here is never simply the result of human willpower but can, finally, only be motivated by and rooted in a radically religious experience.

If the candidate considers this further presumption before he is ready, he might be frightened and even overwhelmed by the prospect of perpetuity. From this perspective, permanence is usually viewed quantitatively: how many long years must I be faithful? A sign of readiness for such presumption is the developing realization that though quantity of years *is* somehow involved, what is more important is a quality and depth of self-realization and of faith experience of God's love. Without such a developed awareness and capacity, an intentional presumption of permanence and perpetuity will not fit the candidate's experience—he is just not ready. The quality of his human and spiritual experience will not have the suppleness and tensile strength needed to hold firm under the weight of perpetuity.

Though this presumption of permanence cannot be made too early, backing it up too close to diaconate ordination also destroys its effectiveness. Ideally, the presumption spoken of here should be made at least a year or two before diaconate ordination.

This timing is true for a very important reason. Such an intentional acceptance of God's presumption of permanent priestly vocation facilitates a final period of discerning that not only further clarifies God's call in the heart of the candidate but also gives him important lived experience of what his daily life will be from ordination until death. The mistake of attempting this presumption too early or too late is surpassed in seriousness only by one other possibility: not to have exercised such an intentional presumption at all before ordination. In this case the candidate does not learn the important process of living discerningly in the light of a God-given identity and mission, a process that is meant to become the very inner structure of his life after ordination. The priest himself will feel this loss over time. Worst of all, the people to be served always suffer most from a lack of decisive and enthusiastic living of a permanent priestly commitment.

To make this presumption in the middle of theological studies is not some artificial "practice" of living like a priest. Were it to seem so unreal and artificial, this would be a sure sign that the candidate is not ready. No, the issue here is serious, and the stakes are high. The clear approval of the candidate in the external forum by the seminary rector and formation staff is expected as part of the process leading up to this special internal exercise of presumption. It is a serious moment of crystallized awareness in the candidate's relationship with Jesus the High Priest. This is no play-acting ruse. With the help of his spiritual director, the candidate recognizes not only his heart's readiness but, even more, its desire for such a special exercise of his relationship with God. He does not feel perfectly in control now of his priestly vocation; rather, the quality of his experiential love relationship with the Risen Jesus is such that the candidate, aware of the high stakes, desires to rely on that love, whatever fear may be quaking in his heart at the prospect of such fidelity.

The actual performance of this presumptive act before God will be a private matter between the candidate and Jesus. It should be planned and staged so as to express its importance and significance in an intimately personal way. Whether it is done after the great central act of communion at Eucharist or in quiet prayer in his candlelit room, it is a moment to be ritualized and journaled with great care. It is a day that stands out in the ordinary events of life, a special touchstone along the journey to priesthood, an experience to be revisited often and meant to provide guidance long into the future. The candidate's heart has settled on a rudder for balance, a compass for direction that has never been so intentionally acknowledged before. The precise point of this presumption is permanence and perseverance of joyful service in diocesan priestly commitment.

Final Stage of Preparatory Discernment

This exercise of presumption of priestly permanence made in the middle of theological studies brings into focus an important final stage of discernment of priestly vocation. Discernment is the interpretation of all of our interior life, especially its spontaneous dimension, according to an acknowledged, profound identity in Jesus. Before this acknowledgment of profound Christian identity, trustworthy discernment in sifting through and interpreting interior experiences is not possible. The process of developing a more refined discernment as we clarify and deepen our identity in Christ is gradual for us all. The next chapter will describe in more detail this process of discernment in the life of the priest. The candidate's life now, especially until ordination, is a matter of prayerfully sorting through daily experiences in presumption of permanent priestly identity and ministry.

This presumption of priestly permanence till death has implications that the candidate must be courageous enough to recognize and live. The rudder of such presumptive priestly identity provides guidance in interpretation that gives clear direction to life. In an even more important way, this daily interpretation deepens priestly intimacy with Jesus and insures faithful presence and service in the midst of the people. This presumptive stand for priestly fidelity will reveal the consoling synchronicity of some inner experiences as the continuing call of God, which, when followed, will deepen priestly identity. The same presumptive stand will reveal the desolate dissonance of other inner experiences as the disquieting influence of an unholy spirit deceptively leading one away from God's priestly call. When these latter experiences are honestly interpreted and courageously resisted, the candidate's priestly identity, once again, deepens.

Presumably, the major part of the candidate's busy daily life will reveal the consoling consistency of his inner life with his priestly vocation. His desire for and satisfaction with such a life and ministry will expand and refine his heart. Vocational temptation cannot be absolutely avoided, however. It is an important dimension of the development of any person's vocation in Christ and is rooted in the divided nature of human consciousness and of all reality. The candidate, at times, will find his feelings tugging—perhaps even straining—against his priestly presumption. In this way his priestly vocation and identity are being tested and purified. Honest interpretation and courageous resistance will help him to believe in God's call beyond what he is now feeling. Without the rudder or compass of his personalized presumption for priestly permanence, such interpretation is much less sure, if possible at all. A man can easily fall prey to the swells and shifts of inner mood and emotions and thereby lose his balance, whereas a well-recognized and personally grasped norm can prevent a fundamental feeling of defenselessness. His intentional self-identification in the presumption for priestly permanence can keep him upright in the buffeting of life's stormy seasons.

As mentioned earlier, discerning from such a priestly presumption will be very instructive for the candidate in this last stage of preparation before ordination. To have experienced the fittingness of this priestly presumption in the course of his development over the years will reveal, in the majority of cases, an even greater clarity and humble confidence about his priestly call. Such a candidate clearly recognizes this readiness and confidently requests acceptance for ordination. This readiness has been facilitated by spiritual direction, by the whole formation process, and especially by his practice of this final priestly presumption. Much less risk accompanies a petition for orders when the candidate is aware of, and relishes, the "feel" of the permanence of priestly commitment.

On the other hand, this intentional presumption can also force the issue of a lack of basic peace and contentment in the priestly call. An ongoing onslaught of inner experiences against priestly commitment prevents the basic joy and contentment needed for lifelong priestly service. In this case, honest interpretation and courageous resistance, as a matter of fact, do not buttress the priestly presumption made. What the candidate may have wanted in some vague but untested way now proves not to hold. What I speak of here is not just one crisis or another but a pattern of discontent over the remaining years before ordination. Usually signs of such discontent will also have appeared previously. In cases such as this, the intentional presumption of priestly permanence has crystallized the awareness that God is not calling this man to perpetual diocesan commitment. Such a person leaves the seminary with a clarity and peace that allow him to follow wherever God is now leading. This clarity is a more welcome blessing before ordination than after.

Ordination: The Presumption Ecclesiastically Ratified

Seminary preparation is not simply directed toward the exciting event of ordination but rather toward the lifelong identity and ministry of priesthood. Though priestly ordination as an event of self-congratulation can, at times, disturbingly assume too selfish an importance and thus distract from the whole identity and ministry of priestly service, nonetheless, the petition for and conferral of orders is obviously a major step in the journey of seminary preparation. As described already, the whole process of presumption of permanent priestly vocation brings the candidate to a humble, confident, and informed petition for ordination to priesthood. This petition is sanctioned by the seminary staff, led by its rector, and ratified by the approving applause of the local people from whom the candidate has been chosen. The whole process of seminary formation, aided by internal and external forums in their own distinctive ways and dramatized in the lived presumption of diocesan priestly permanence, finally brings the man to approval for ordination.

GEORGE A. ASCHENBRENNER, S.J.

The rite of priestly ordination is an act of God in and through the church. In this way the candidate's presumption of priestly vocation and perseverance, which has grown throughout his seminary years, is now validated publicly in the church. Obviously this action is never done impulsively or without careful consideration of compelling evidence. It is an action rich in revelation: for God, revealed as gloriously transforming Love; for this local presbyterate, in its special role of revealing that Love; for the new priest himself, now empowered to be a special priestly enfleshment of that Love; and finally for the people, served in invitation to their own unique radiating of God's glorious love in Jesus. This day, deserving full and grand celebration throughout the whole church, should also imprint itself deeply on the heart of the newly ordained. A whole future life of faithful ministry is powerfully poised in this event.

This ecclesial ratification of the presumption of God's call to permanent priestly identity and ministry gives assurance and encouraging clarification for the rest of the new priest's life. This assimilated presumption, though very helpful for the new priest, is not enough just by itself to get him through the transition of the first few years. Gatherings of new priests sponsored by the presbyterate, the mentoring help of a senior priest, and the honest encouragement of parishioners are meant to complement the new priest's personal preparation. The priest's presumption is now even more public than when done in the seminary and is not just some private devotion between himself and Jesus. As publicly ratified in the church, it has a certitude and clarity that can stay with the priest through the rest of his ministry. This presumption, tested and ever more personally assimilated over the years, now stands as a rudder, a compass, a beacon giving light, balance, and direction for the future. The last few years of training have especially fit this rudder to the "feel" of the new priest's heart. His gaze has been focused on that beacon, and he has learned to read that compass.

Now his priestly life with all its rich and exciting variety will be enlightened in the daily presumption of permanent priestly ordination. The discernment experienced previously in line with his presumption of priestly permanence is an invaluable aid in his daily life. Whatever in his interior life further reveals and deepens his priestly identity is presumed to be of God's Holy Spirit, whether it involves obvious joy and satisfaction or invites him to a painful, difficult challenge. Whatever deceptively interferes with his priestly call, whether a mood of happy feelings or a burdensome feeling of boredom and failure, is now interpreted as the temptation of an unholy spirit. Following the guidance of God's Spirit in resisting the deceptive insinuations of the evil spirit becomes very practical and concrete. Insightful courage and trust in God's promise of a faithful priestly call become the issue at hand. Now the young priest who falls in love presumes that this is not a call away from priestly commitment. Rather, the issue is what kind of relationship, if any, he is to welcome with this woman. The priest who is bored and losing the glow of his priestly commitment presumes he is not being called away from priestly ministry but must rather investigate means to renew himself and rekindle the fire of his permanent priestly identity. This presumption of priestly permanence is paramount in the new priest's heart and provides vocational interpretation in every situation. He has learned this over years of growth into intentional identification with this presumption of priestly permanence.

This identification of self with presumptive priestly perseverance is not an exercise of superego or some Kantian moral imperative. As mentioned earlier, this presumption is rooted in an ever developing experience of God's intimate, enlightening love in Jesus. This experience of the fire of love in Jesus' heart that rooted and revealed the man's priestly vocation in the first place must continue to grow in the intimacy of prayer and discernment. Otherwise the ratified priestly presumption of permanence will lose its radiance. No superego empowers the priestly presumption. It is the continuing ignition and flame of a love affair with God in the beauty of Jesus the High Priest. This priestly presumption is not to be clung to irrationally or blindly; rather, there is the clarity and power of vocational commitment radiating from a love that will stake all in relying on the Beloved's promise to be faithful and to guide us always.

Conclusion

The presumption of priestly permanence presented here should play a central role in seminary preparation. If the candidate does learn such a presumption, it will make a difference in his preparation for petition for priestly ordination. It will also aid him in the joys and trials of priestly ministry.

What I am speaking of is no magic wand with which a priest waves his way through his ministry or some unbreakable walking stick clung to for dear life. The presumption this chapter has described is meant to become the inner structure of the priestly candidate's heart, a heart becoming more and more inflamed in God's attractive love as revealed in Jesus. This inner drive of love, enlightened and eager to be faithful to God's glorious dream for the whole universe, always finds focus for a diocesan priest in fidelity to a particular local people. This presumed fidelity requires the courage to stand firm in a promise and profession unto death, just as Jesus did, especially on Calvary, where the light and hope of resurrection originally dawned slowly and now burns with a permanent radiance.

A Discerning Presence in the Midst of a Local People

Holiness, in and of itself, does not seem to be a serious daily concern for most people. A second thought makes us wonder about this apparent lack of concern. Often stated in other words and with a deceptive indirectness, the longing of the human heart for more than it knows and possesses now does stir in all of us in quiet daily moments. When the glow has faded from life and something is clearly missing, this search for something more is really a desire for fullness, for beauty, for God, even though we do not know it and cannot articulate it as such. In many ways the ordinary people of a parish feel and express what really is a desire for holiness, for a relationship that gets them out of the narrow confines of their own selves. They are seeking greater meaning, more happiness, and greater love in the daily routine of their lives. Other people on the parish scene are more explicit and direct. They want to pray better; they want to know God's love more; they want their faith to be more alive.

Though a counselor or a friend might sometimes be approached to help with these concerns, the principal local person to whom these daily stirrings and longings are brought is the diocesan priest. People look to him for help, for answers, for the solution to their dissatisfaction. But what can the priest do? What answers does he have?

In this chapter I will develop more fully the charism discussed in chapter 6 of the diocesan priest as a discerning presence in the midst of a local people. I will also explicate in more detail the rigorous, revelatory discernment made possible by the presumption for priestly permanence and perseverance described in the previous chapter. The graced art of daily growth in holiness is precisely what we mean by *discernment of spirits*. It is a very human process of inspiration, enlightening us to interpret the fire of God's awesome love flaming in our daily human experience. The human psyche is always encountering our loving God in a variety of ways. These encounters are both profoundly human and much more than human; they are faith experiences of a love promising a joy that alone can satisfy us to some real extent here and now and in a complete way on the other side of death. This discerned art of holiness is not a matter of learning a catalog of answers and then distributing them on request. Rather, it is a life to be lived in the uniquely personal part of our hearts, a life that must also extend an invitation for union with all of our human brothers and sisters in the transformation of our entire expanding universe.

This chapter is not meant to be a mini-course on discernment, nor is it a review of the answers the priest will need for all the people's questions. I want to present some of what is involved in the priest's understanding and living of discernment, so centrally involved as it is in his radiating the fire of the Holy Spirit for the parish people. After presenting a four-step process that constitutes a discerning life, I will briefly describe three dimensions of human existence that are always the stage on which the drama of a personal love-relationship with God plays itself out. As a spiritual leader in the midst of the parish, the priest must have a reflective understanding of the art of discernment, seen as the dynamic of any mature faith life. This charism prepares the priest to play two important roles of service in the midst of the people: a guide into the mystery of God's fire of love and a soul doctor for those being healed and purified in that same fire.

Discernment: God's Story of Mature Faith Growth

Holiness and growth in union with God always involve the full human person alive in the present concrete situation of the world. A person's spiritual maturity does involve good actions and the full range of human emotions, but it also involves a lot more. With concern for actions and feelings, spiritual maturity also cuts into the inner core and foundation of a person. This core focuses the lenses of action and feeling for a clear picture of God's love radiating, whether brilliantly or behind clouds, through the whole world. The invitation is to recognize and welcome this love in every situation, and discernment of spirits is the means to such recognition.

Sometimes discernment is mistakenly seen as one of any number of approaches, instead of the only approach, to mature spiritual development. Indeed, some schools of thought on faith development do have their own terminology for describing their perspective and approach. However, at the root of these different articulations is one fundamental process that is always involved in mature faith growth, a process of sorting our inner experiences, a process of discerning spirits. For this reason discernment of spirits is *the* story—God's story—of personal faith growth. This process is doubly rooted in our reality as human beings created by God and in the revelation of Jesus. Discernment of spirits is God's only story of personal faith growth, narrated both in our very makeup as human creatures and in God's revelation of interpersonal love for us all in Jesus. If only this interpersonal love shone clearly, brilliantly, beautifully in every situation! At times, it does. At other times, the radiance of this love is shadowed by the pollution of a thin smog or, even worse, by a heavy cloud of evil that stains our beautiful world and infects our human bloodstream. If all were goodness, grace, and beauty, how wonderful things would be. There would be no need for careful sorting in such a good world. Conversely, if all were evil, darkness, and wickedness, we would teeter on the brink of despair—but, again, there would be no need for any sorting.

In a world in which the human condition is unavoidably ambiguous and mixed, however, a discernment of sorting out the variety of spirits in our hearts assumes an essential importance if we are not only to discover but also to display in our very person the glory of love in our daily lives. The dictionary tells us that to discern is to sort and separate out. When this is put in the human context of faith and spirituality, the sorting and separating concerns the mixture of inner spirits in our hearts, the act of distinguishing the dark, evil, overly selfish impulses from the glorious, radiant inspirations of the Holy Spirit of God. For many people, this sorting of spirits is not always done with a reflective awareness. If it is not done at all, mature faith eludes them. As mentioned earlier, the priest as spiritual leader and soul doctor in the parochial community must do the hard work and undergo the serious training needed for an intelligent, experiential grasp of this art of discerned holiness and soul doctoring.

In the midst of such careful inner sorting, we must never forget that God desires and is committed to each of us in Jesus more than we can fully realize before death, and the Holy Spirit is constantly active in our hearts and in our world. Christian holiness always has its initiative in the fire of God's loving desire for us. It is never a figment of our imagination or a product of our willpower. It is the mystery of God's precious gift for us all. Each of us must learn to recognize, receive, and nurture the gift. We need a guide to lead us, in some special ways, into the fire, into the radiant glow of the mystery of God's love burning bright in Jesus.

The Material of Discernment

The great challenge and invitation that haunts us all is to discover our true selves in Christ. For each of us, God purposefully intends a unique revelation of Christ. Though the enterprise has very complex aspects, the point is as simple as it is startling: God intends a unique imitation of Jesus on the part of each one of us. We are meant to live this unique imitation of Christ and, beyond the enclosure of our own lives, to shine for all the world.

This true self, the treasure of this unique revelation, is camouflaged in the spontaneous interiority of our daily consciousness. This pearl of great price must be searched for and recognized when stumbled upon. In the daily spontaneous consciousness of the priest and of his people, hordes of images, feelings, thoughts, impulses, and moods stealthily insinuate themselves or, at other times, shockingly surprise. This inner spontaneous world has a variety of seasons. The spring of our hearts can be bright, scintillating, and uplifting, but winter can seem heavy, dark, and frightening. We might wish that the treasure of our true self in Christ be delivered more directly and easily so we would not have to wade into this marsh of spontaneity within ourselves, but there is no "guaranteed overnight delivery." God takes the complexity of our human condition very seriously, so this unique revelation of Jesus does not come in some startling, inhuman apparition, but must be sought in the entanglements of the encounter between the concrete situation of today's historical world and our own consciousness. To refuse to enter this lively encounter is to deprive ourselves—and all others—of the unique revelation of Christ as intended by God through our lives. This is life without the radiance of fire. Whenever one person decides not to enter this struggle, the radiance of us all is somehow dimmed. The diocesan priest, this soul doctor, as part of his special role in the midst of the people, cannot avoid the search for the hidden treasure, because when it is discovered and owned, its glow will radiate far beyond himself.

This discerning search for the treasure of our true selves can be synthesized in a four-step process. As I briefly describe this process, it is important to remember that in the stress of daily life, these four elements are not as simple and clear as here presented. My intention is to describe this process in a way that will help the priest to recognize it in his own experience and thus to understand it more personally and explicitly. Then this discerning process can help the priestly soul doctor to guide people in discovering and welcoming the mystery of God's love in their hearts and lives.

Turned toward God

The first element, which is very profound and important, concerns our identity in Jesus Christ. Until this identity has been cultivated, serious discernment is not possible. A serious turning to God seeds the heart's soil for discernment and in this way initiates any trustworthy searching for the treasure of God's uniquely personal love. This turning over of the soil, this cultivation, is a real conversion that grades the ground of our heart to a new incline, away from ourselves and toward God. It is more than a passing fancy or a momentary quirk. The realization that we are conceived, marked, and shaped from the dawn of our existence by a God who always and only loves us strikes root and shifts the contour and landscape of our daily lives. This realization of a Love that is greater than the love we have for ourselves stops us in our tracks. It invites an about-face and gets us out of ourselves. A whole new vista opens up. We have discovered and been turned toward Someone more beloved than we are to ourselves. Is this Love for real? Can this Beloved be trusted? What are we to make of it all? As this flurry of early sproutings appears in the soil and we decide to cultivate them, the realization can come that receiving and responding to such Love assumes an importance beyond all else. The ground under our feet shakes and radically shifts.

At this juncture, it is clear to others and to ourselves that something has changed. A central question has been posing itself in our hearts for a long time: Am I the ultimate meaning of my own life? In hearing that question, the winds of our contemporary culture howl an answer: "Yes, of course!" and the blustery air of this culture blows its way into our bloodstream, as it has persistently done in the past. "Of course I am the ultimate meaning of my own life! If not I, who else could be?" But now that *yes* is radically shaken and on the verge of being splintered into a *no*. The seeds of self-love and self-acceptance are now more carefully inspected and then sown as part of the soil's cultivation. The rooting of the tree of our lives is changed. "The ultimate meaning of my own life? No, it is not I myself. God's Love is—as promised and present in the Risen Jesus." A new sun has risen, and it will never set. Now life increasingly becomes a fascination with this mysterious Beloved and with radical openness and readiness for whatever that Love radiates.

Something has deepened and developed. An early seedling of religious intuition became the fragile sprouting of a realization that, when tested in the wind of culture, has become a deep rooting. Over time, an early surmise and semiconscious intuition has become a resolute desire of will. No tall grass shivering in the wind, this tree is deeply rooted and capable now of new growth. This resolute desire shapes and casts our lives in love: first in God's ever-faithful love in the Risen Jesus and then in our own love as a carefully discerned response. From now on life will be about love, at times tough love, but love nonetheless. Make no mistake about that! In some important way we are no longer in charge of our own lives. God is! Life is not yes to self but yes to God as radiant in Jesus (2 Corinthians 1:19, "with him it was always Yes").

Facing Our Spontaneous Life

Insofar as the countercultural movement toward God's love has begun to take serious root in our hearts, a second step beckons. Only honest facing of our inner spontaneous life makes possible a trustworthy interpretation for God in faith. As correct and logical as this statement is, it prescinds from the ingenuity of human consciousness for dishonest avoidance and selfish projection.

We must learn, as best we can, to stand clear of these deceptions, whether conscious or unconscious, if we are to discern God's loving desire in our hearts. This element in itself is no easy matter, and it invites the priest to an asceticism leading to truth and love. Sometimes this asceticism, always motivated by a growing desire for the concreteness of God's consoling love, will involve something as difficult as unlearning a previous training. An overly rational view of Christian spirituality downplays, and even scorns, the role of spontaneity and feeling, whereas a supersensitivity to sentiment can smuggle into Christian spirituality, a presumption that proclaims, sometimes quite unwittingly, that whatever we feel is God's will for us. In both of these instances a previous learning must be honestly acknowledged, judged as incorrect, and gradually changed. As difficult as this change may seem, especially when the previously learned viewpoint has taken deep root, such a conversion is always possible for two reasons: God steadfastly desires to get through to us, and our own soul desires greater radiance. If the priest stays in close touch with these two desires, he will be capable of whatever transformation is

GEORGE A. ASCHENBRENNER, S.J.

necessary, because it will be the work of the radiant Holy Spirit of God beckoning him beyond his own depth and into the realm of greater mystery in faith.

A Wisdom of Interpretation in Faith

In the process of discernment I am describing here, for someone clearly turned toward God and honestly sensitive to the flow of inner spontaneity, the issue becomes a matter of meaning. The spontaneous experience of the moment, resonating within and honestly acknowledged, always poses the question of meaning for one turned toward God. Where is God in all of this? The answer to this question requires a certain wisdom and interpretive ability. The interpretation could spring from any number of different vantage points, such as lived common sense, the majority cultural opinion, professional theories of human development, or Christian faith. All of these different "wisdoms" might overlap to a small or large extent, but each would produce a different conclusion when used as the central focus of interpretation. In discernment the focus is profoundly one of decisive Christian faith, radiating with the experience of Jesus Christ and revealed in the Holy Spirit. How God is present here and now, offering a love beyond all loves: that is the central concern for a person turned toward and identified in God.

As we have seen already, God is always present but never simply and completely in all of our present historical world or in all of our spontaneous inner experience. That treasure of a love beyond all value, that revelation of our own unique imitation of Jesus must be sought in the mixture and confusion of our inner lives. An enlightenment of the Holy Spirit rooted in and springing from our experience of God's faithful love alone—what we called in chapter 3 a monasticism of the heart—is the gift needed at this point. Such enlightenment and wisdom differ subtly but sharply from enthusiastic generosity and simplistic sincerity. By themselves, without graced wisdom, these two qualities lack a built-in North Star and can be dangerously misleading. The wisdom referred to here has a profound paschal orientation and is found more and more decisively present and operative in Jesus as he moves into the depths of his passion. This wisdom and enlightenment are not the result of an academic course or of reading a book. It is a grace for which the priest regularly prays.

Such paschal wisdom in faith is not some sleight of hand or based on guesswork. The process described here contextualizes this wisdom and helps the priest to recognize and receive this gifted insight. The Spirited interpretation sought results from a testing of our feelings and experience against the lodestone of our deep-hearted identity in God's love. The presence of the Holy Spirit is revealed in anything that conforms to our determined desire of will to keep God's love, not self, at our center. Anything that violates this resolute identity by putting us back at the center is not an inspiration from God but a nudge, however slight or overt, toward self-idolatry.

A pleasure-pain instinct strongly brands our affectivity and orients us all toward self-idolatry. This instinct for liking pleasure and fearing pain is understandable and healthy. When we let it assume a priority and centrality such that it usurps the chief focal light for our interpretation, however, then we become narcissistic. This pleasure-pain principle, in and of itself, is never fully identified with the paschal enlightenment of God's love, nor was it so identified in the experience of Jesus. The pleasure-pain instinct did not map his way to his beloved Father. An important asceticism is involved in escaping the dominance of this instinct. We are not to renounce this instinct pure and simple; rather, we renounce it as the North Star of our identity. Developing our interpersonal faith relationship of love with God in the beauty of Jesus will not completely uproot this instinct, but it does take some of the bite out of it. God's love in Jesus has become the treasure beyond all value, and what a grace it is to know indescribable pain when deprived of that treasure. To learn how to stand with Jesus, sometimes in pleasure, at other times in pain, is the mature wisdom of a person planted more and more in the ground of God's love. It is to discover and claim that treasure intended by God before the foundation of the world: a radiant true self uniquely imitating the mystery of Jesus.

Tactics for Intimacy with God

The final step in this process is the application of decisive tactics in accord with the paschal faith-interpretation of the previous step. For someone whose heart is resolutely set on following God's love, anything experienced as an incarnation of that love (often called *consolation*) is to be embraced, claimed, and followed. Anything that deflects from one's resolute desire for God's love and moves one toward self-idolatry (usually called *desolation*) is to be rejected and courageously withstood. At this point in the process, the issue is courage and decisive generosity, which are only possible as they are enlightened and energized by the inspiration of paschal wisdom. A whole armory of tactics exists for responding to the paschal interpretation. At this conclusion of the process, whether the spontaneity is of God or not is not the issue. That is known. Now the issue is whether or not, and how wholeheartedly, we will follow the revelation of the Holy Spirit. Here character of soul is doctored, and heroism of faith is humbly forged in the fire of the Holy Spirit.

A Hidden Self Grown Strong

As this process takes on the integration and flow of a life, a person grows into and lives a mature, discerning faith. This process also plays itself out in three different dimensions of our human person and, finally, invites an integration that roots the treasure of God's revelation in a hidden self grown strong.[1] As this chapter draws to a close, I will briefly describe this further development of the priest's charism of being a discerning presence in the midst of the people.

In a life of mature spirituality, discernment always acknowledges, distinguishes, and then interrelates three different dimensions of human existence: external behavior, inner spontaneity, and what I call the core of the soul. To live out of a developed core sense of true self is never easy, especially in our postmodern world, but it is always crucial to responsible, mature living in faith. Our contemporary culture has great need of doctors of the soul who can facilitate the development of this core sense of true self through the integration of these three dimensions of human existence. The first dimension is behavioral and external. This observable aspect of our person, though it often consumes enormous amounts of energy, constitutes a superficial part of our being. The activity dramatized on this stage poses a question of meaning that it cannot answer by itself. In the drama of our daily activity we touch and influence many people, and the New Testament reminds us that the activity of sincere loving reveals the genuineness of our faith. In the midst of our busy lives, one question often echoes in our hearts: Are we simply what we do? Some careful reflection is needed to answer correctly, lest we squander the depths and shrink the roots of our human faith life, misleading ourselves and others by limiting its full significance to this superficial, obvious reality.

A second dimension of our person throbs its way into our attention. I call this very real area of rational or affective spontaneity the "skin" of the soul. As mentioned earlier, this experience of spontaneity is the field that conceals the deeply seeded treasure of our true self in Christ. These spontaneities of thinking and feeling skitter their way across the skin of our souls but never strike to the core. Impulses, images, and moods can rage across our minds with the intensity of an electrical storm and seem to come and go with a bedeviling arbitrariness that frustrates and enrages us. These spontaneities are neither profound nor permanent, and they do, finally, pass. This dimension of spontaneous, unintentional experience is characterized by the unpredictability of shifting sands and is not capable of the rocklike dependability of the core of the soul.

This skin-of-the-soul dimension poses its own question: Are we simply and wholly identified by what we spontaneously think or feel? Though what we feel is never equal to who we are, we can easily be swept into a false judgment in the deluge of a temporary storm. My point here is simple: these spontaneities happen on a different level of our person. They play a real and important role in the process of integration that is human and spiritual maturity, but they find their direction only in relation to the soul's core.

In the core of the soul, the final dimension reflected on here, we encounter the utterly unique, deepest part of every human person. This core of the soul plays a crucial role in the process of discovering our true self in the beauty of Christ. A deep-hearted personal world, a treasure beyond value, is gradually revealed, acknowledged, and laid claim to, though this whole process is much more received than of our own making. This inner core has a depth and a simplicity that is beyond words. As we grow in our appreciation of this personal center, its presence dawns, alluringly shrouded in mystery. Such mysteriousness does not imply cloudy ambiguity. Rather, within the shifting mists of this inner mysterious realm, a noisy world hushes into a resounding quiet. In this core of our soul God's creative love is breathing the gift of life into us moment by moment, now, and on into eternity. It is this same creative love, unique to each of us, that breathes life into every person. As we are led ever deeper into the core of our soul, our experience of God and of ourselves becomes more profound, personal, and unique.

This deepest core speaks of the infinite simplicity and love of God which, even as you now read, is breathing life into you. This profoundly personal inner experience, this quiet conversation of love at our deepest core, belies the deadening loneliness that sometimes seems to suck away the breath of our life. This profoundly personal experience of love, concentrated like a laser beam of goodness at our deepest center, also belies the illusion of anyone's being rotten to the core. There is in each of us a deepest central point where evil cannot reach and where only the beauty of God's creative love exists in all its uniqueness. A buried treasure, a pearl beyond price, a hidden self revealed in Jesus waits to be discovered, to be embraced, and to grow strong.

The dynamics involved in integrating these three dimensions of our person and how the four-step process of discernment plays itself out in this integration should be very familiar to the priest.[2] They represent the heart and soul of living a mature, discerning faith. To let the limpid core interpret and give direction to the spontaneities of the skin and, finally, to enliven this integration in appropriate action is to live a mature faith, an effort that is sometimes easy and obvious and at other times is confusing and excruciating. Both the ecstasy and the agony of living God's deepest truth of love in our unique imitation of Jesus teach and encourage us.

The core of the soul and the skin of the soul, acting out their interpretation: this is the realm of service for a doctor of the soul. The next chapter further highlights aspects of the priest's distinctive soul-doctoring work. In his service of their souls the priest guides his people into the awareness that all our lives are shrouded in mystery—the mystery of God, whose fire of soul-love radiates from the face of Jesus the High Priest.

Minister of God's Loving Forgiveness

In the beginning of the last chapter I referred to a variety of ways in which the desire for holiness takes expression on the part of many people in a parish. Often, this longing for holiness, however variously expressed, centers on forgiveness. The tangled and frayed edges of human encounters leave us bruised, scarred, guilt ridden, and trembling in a lack of peace. This is no dramatic, public experience. Rather, it takes place in the quiet of our private lives, where the stress and strain of hearts quivering in guilt and blushing with flashes of shame deprive us of a deep peace. All of this reveals a sometimes desperate need to forgive and be forgiven. Though we quickly learn how to distract ourselves from these inner messages, they will not go away. In some deep quiet way we know that we are not at home with ourselves. Forgiveness—the forgiveness of God—is at the heart of Christian holiness.

In chapter 5, I presented as one of the charisms of diocesan priesthood the priest's role as minister of God's loving forgiveness in the midst of the parish. Exercising this charism is part of the distinctive spirituality unique to diocesan priesthood. It is another way in which this doctor of the soul calls down fire from heaven, a fire that burns, purifies, heals, and bestows a zealous ministerial peace. In this chapter I will develop a bit of what this central charism requires of the diocesan priest.

A program of priestly formation has an important role to play in the priest's preparation for service as special minister of God's loving forgiveness. In addition to the important canonical and moral aspects of this preparation, a profound spirituality inflames the whole experience. A complex of interrelated dynamics, a whole journey with many stages[1] is involved and must be learned. A contemporary academic, intellectual learning must be integrated with an important experiential dimension. To ask whether or not the priest is a good confessor is really to ask if he is a good forgiver. This question, while pointing clearly to the sacrament of reconciliation, stretches far beyond that rite. The priest, as minister of God's forgiveness, enacts a forgiving presence in the midst of the local people, a presence that is related to the discerning presence discussed in the previous chapter. The dynamics involved in receiving God's forgiveness require a careful inner discernment.

In this chapter I will describe some of the stages of the journey of God's forgiveness with its many implications for the diocesan priest-minister. There is a dynamic process necessarily involved if the graced reception of God's precious forgiveness in Christ Jesus is to deliver on its promise of new life in the radical transformation of our souls. We are concerned here with a journey of grace within the human heart, aimed at nothing less than new life and a transformation of soul. Forgiveness opens the gates to and reveals that treasure beyond price, that unique imitation of Jesus intended by God for each of us. The dynamics described here will help the priest in his service as soul doctor, not only in the formal sacrament but also in a more informal ministering of God's forgiveness in his mutual interaction with the people in the sacramentality of their daily lives.

Reflective Awareness Required

For the forgiving love of God to reconcile the heart of an individual or of a whole community, time and the careful cooperation of believing persons are required. God's reconciling forgiveness never happens in us all at once or in utter disregard of our own dispositions. A subtle analysis can produce a reflective awareness that will facilitate a profoundly renewing experience of the fire of God's forgiveness and thus lay foundations for an ever more profound, grateful, and decisive commitment to the mystery of Christ. The priest's ministerial role of calling down fire from heaven for the doctoring of souls requires that he have his own personal understanding of this analysis and its resulting reflective awareness. Such analysis is obviously not essential for everyone who celebrates and receives God's forgiveness, nor is it meant to make the priest or the penitents overly self-conscious.

Perhaps the greatest danger in such analysis is an apparent fussiness or legalism—or even worse, an apparent control and manipulation of the gloriously gratuitous mystery of God. With an eternity, a freedom, and a fullness that will always stagger our earthbound consciousness, God will be God, far beyond any effort of ours. In the beauty of Jesus, the attractiveness of God's infinitely creative mercy invites our human response to be part of that great mystery of glorification revealed for the fullness of time. As a result, from our human perspective, what in God may be eternally full and entire becomes in us a gradual appropriation over time. In describing this gradual dynamic of our experience I will follow the lead of the Scriptures in using some anthropomorphic language to describe the mysterious and necessary interaction of the divine and the human. This human language is never meant to limit the divine fullness and glory, but rather to allow the divine reality to far surpass and outshine any human expression used here.

Through his reflective awareness the priest becomes a catechist of the human heart for his people. Such a catechist helps the people to understand—to read the signs and to respond to the pace of God's forgiving Spirit in their hearts. In order to come to such an understanding, a much greater reflective awareness is needed of the graced dynamics provoked in the human heart by the Holy Spirit of God's forgiveness. If we can all come to appreciate more the interconnectedness of many of our inner experiences in life, and if we can understand how these moods and movements of heart are part of a divinely intended inner journey, then we will cooperate more gracefully with God's infinitely forgiving love. As a result, the fire of God's mercy in Christ Jesus can transform each of us into the steady flame of a joyous peace and a passionate concern for loving justice.

The experiences presented here are so profoundly personal that they bridge the social and the private, the communal and the individual. My reflections are not meant to imply a priority for either the individual form of the sacrament or a combination of individual and communal forms. Rather, the stages of the inner journey of forgiveness undercut that issue by providing a substratum of development that is the basis for the integration of the two forms. Though my reflections are primarily concerned with an experience in the heart of the individual believer, I am always presuming the church's full communal and social understanding of the mystery of sin and of God's loving forgiveness in Christ Jesus.

From beginning to end, in all aspects of this experience and even in those phases that offend and shock our natural, unconverted sensibility (how different the viewpoint of the saints!), the fire of God's love invites and challenges us insistently into the deep glow of peace and the radiant energy of salvation in Christ Jesus. In much of this experience our affectivity is jolted by the sting of guilt, the singe of shame, the hurt of humiliation. These are not pleasurable experiences! But they are nonetheless an essential part of God's inviting us deeper into a forgiveness that will purify us in renewed peace and joy. Before any second thought or reflection, these painful experiences spontaneously seek camouflage in pleasurable distraction. In terms of the pleasure-pain instinct, these experiences repel us rather than entice us. A careful discernment is needed to sort out these charged affections so as to recognize where and how grace beckons us. This kind of doctoring of the soul and catechizing of the heart require a reflective, personal familiarity on the priest's part if he is to help the people.

A First Feeling Bad about Self

Many people today feel bad about themselves. They do not like themselves. Often it is not their fault that this gloom has been inflicted upon them. Living with such dislike of self is too painful on a daily basis, so they try to forget it and self-dramatize in a pleasant, happy, or even arrogant persona. Such a mask is paper thin and cannot conceal, much less heal, the inner heartache. Inside, they are still contorted by the pain of a self-dislike that can verge on self-disdain or even self-hatred.

GEORGE A. ASCHENBRENNER, S.J.

For someone in a primitive state of unreflectiveness, these dynamics of dislike can shackle the soul. One must take a step up from primitive, spiritual obliviousness to begin a serious life in the Spirit. A person's pre-evangelized identity cannot make sense of or get free from the clutches of self-dislike. People will remain spiritually primitive until a need or desire for some reflective slowing down and questioning of their natural spontaneity grows in their hearts. All sorts of life experiences, whether dramatically critical or boringly ordinary, can frustrate and dissatisfy enough to provoke this need or desire for greater reflection on the spiritual meaning of life. As the spiritually primitive person stirs out of unreflectiveness and moves toward greater seriousness, precisely what is needed is light, the light of fire, an enlightenment in faith. Evangelization in the radiance of the Holy Spirit provides this discerning enlightenment.

This first feeling bad about self, which is quite different, as we will see, from a second similar feeling, lacks the exhilaration of grace and of the Holy Spirit. The dark discouragement of being trapped in self bespeaks a very different spirit. An important early element of Christian evangelization for the primitive person is this realization that every human heart and all of reality is haunted by a dark, evil, and demonic spirit that always enticingly counsels the opposite of God's love. These primitive people, so down on themselves because they have been victimized, chiefly by not being loved, are feeling the desolate presence of this dark spirit. This attitude sits in their hearts like a poison and can sour their presence in everything.

These people also often feel plagued by unhealthy guilt and shame. Such people, whose hearts are stifled by anxiety and whose energy is frittered away by a suffocating fear of punishment, keep the focus on themselves, and therefore their guilt is not related to love and trust. This anxious experience of guilt is unhealthy and is not part of the graced touch of God's loving forgiveness. In fact, because it is energized by the demonic spirit, it usually is a disruptive interference. Though not a choice of will and not exactly put in so many words, such shame blankets a person's whole being. A shame concerning who they are stains their whole makeup and forestalls self-confidence and self-esteem. There seems to be nothing about themselves that they can believe in. This shame pollutes the heart in a way that reveals its unhealthiness and its lack of gracefulness. Such shame is not a sign of the Holy Spirit, nor is it the invitation of a forgiving God.

The dingy, polluted dungeon in which these people feel themselves trapped does not have to be an eternal prison. These people can, and often do, recover. Liberation comes in an experience of genuine love, however long it may take to trust and receive such love. This slowly and gradually brings about a whole new life in which the person experiences an invigorating self-esteem. A soul that felt poisoned and rotten slowly begins to etch the lines of a smile. This amazing change is charged with great hope for the future. Often it is *felt* before it is *understood,* and these people must be encouraged to believe in the change that is actually happening, a change that can be as monumental as the difference between a sickening wish for death and a throbbing desire for life. That treasure of a unique imitation of Jesus, the realistic possibility of a true self beloved in Jesus, begins to spark and fascinate the heart as the gloom of the past continues to lift and as love brings to the heart an expansiveness and farsighted vision. Life has a new glow to it—a fire has been kindled.

A Second Feeling Bad about Self

With time, shadows will inevitably dim the glow and crosscurrents will slake the fire. Another way of feeling bad blows across the heart, a feeling that is different from the previous one and warrants careful reflection. The bedfellows of guilt and shame move in again, disrupting the placid, benign goodness of the scene.

An understandable yet dangerous decision could block the careful, clear view needed at this juncture. For someone finally released from the dingy dungeon of self-hatred, for someone now breathing the exhilarating air of love, how right the decision might seem to never again seriously entertain a bad feeling about oneself. This decision would actually be at cross-purposes with maturing in faith, however, as this second feeling bad is the grace of God's love burning into our hearts and revealing the sin of insufficient love in all our lives. If this feeling bad is dismissed, a door to even greater intimacy and union with God is closed.

This time, the guilt and shame have a different tone to them. They are shimmerings of grace, however unpleasantly they register at first. This guilt born of God's forgiveness results from healthy interpersonal love and trust. The commitment of love with the Beloved has been violated, and the violation is recognized as such. This guilt signals the Beloved's presence—a very active presence, a redemptive spirit—and invites greater intimacy in faith with God. When recognized for what it is, this graced guilt, although it stings painfully, focuses the heart beyond itself, on the Beloved, in shame and sorrow for the wound one's lack of love has caused. This shift of focus stirs a different experience, one that acknowledges failure in the behavior rather than shaming the person. Experiencing the Beloved as disappointed and hurt but as still wanting to forgive us scorches us with a shame whose burning purifies and deepens the love relationship with the Beloved.

If, however, in the face of their honestly recognized violation of love and their awareness of the Beloved's full knowledge, people now perceive the Beloved as menacingly searching them out for punishment and destruction, then a quaking, self-protective fear, rather than the purifying sting of shame, rocks their consciousness. This self-centered, anxious fear is not the mature experience of God's loving forgiveness inviting conversion and ongoing transformation, nor is it the fear of the Lord that initiates wisdom. When God's forgiving love, under grace, imposes belief before the witness of the cross, then wonder and amazement confuse the soul. How can someone be so faithful in the face of my infidelity? Why should someone prevent my receiving the punishment that my sinful ingratitude justly deserves? The more seriously and profoundly we encounter the fire of God's love in Christ Jesus, the more our sin is revealed in the burning, purifying, and exhilarating experience of embarrassed shame in the presence of the Beloved of our heart. When standing in this shame and amazement before God's faithful love in Jesus on the cross, we know in our sorrow that we must apologize or there will always be something awkward and unreconciled in our relationship.

Helping to distinguish the attendant subtleties of these two ways of feeling bad about self is an important part of the priest's service as a doctor of the soul guiding the people ever more thoroughly into the mystery of God.

A Flame of Sorrow Is Enkindled

In the contemporary culture of autonomy and independence, apology and sorrow seem weak and cowardly, often embarrassingly so. What good can come from such sorrow and apology? They seem destructive of self-confidence and self-reliance. It is a great contemporary challenge to find energy and fire in the simmering coals of sorrow. Once again, this challenge is part of the diocesan priest's charism as a special forgiving presence, a soul doctor, in the midst of the people.

Sorrow and repentance are important parts of God's gift of forgiving love, but this is often not an easy gift to receive. As part of this gift from God, such sorrow does not disregard human effort, so when we feel deficient in our experience of sorrow, the problem is not in God but somehow in ourselves. To desire a greater sense of sorrow invites us to pray for it, but it must also lead us to certain requisite attitudes and dispositions if we are to receive this grace. To welcome from our God of faithful forgiveness the blessing of profound sorrow for our sins requires at least two fundamental attitudes, each of which can be problematic, especially today.

First, for any mature experience of sorrow, we must know we are genuinely responsible for our sin. Whenever we listen—not simply hear, but also listen—to that evil spirit within us that rationalizes away our responsibility, then the graced experience of shamed sorrow and the accompanying conversion of heart to greater love grow vague and ambiguous. Sometimes, psychological and anthropological difficulties with human freedom and responsibility must be confronted and recognized as leading to an unbelief opposed to the graced invitation of the Risen Jesus

GEORGE A. ASCHENBRENNER, S.J.

to a transformed self as part of God's ministry of forgiving love in our world.

Second, to slip into the illusion that our sin in no way touches or affects God is to prevent much (if not all) experience of sorrow for our sins before God. This second attitude involves a prayerful appreciation of the effect of our sin on God. This is not easy to describe, because neither a childishly uninformed explanation (sin as a slap on God's face) nor an overly secularized, narrowly humanistic explanation (sorrow for sin as something felt with other human beings but not with God) will do. We enter here upon the profound mystery of God as revealed in Christ and as presented through the church's careful theological reflection and articulation. Some of the anthropomorphic language of the Scriptures can help us.

The effect of our sin before our lovingly creative God involves what we might call a moment of disappointment. The Scriptures describe, or at least hint at, an effect of disappointment before God revealed in Jesus Christ, whose forgiving response to our sin is always faithful and full. Because disappointment constitutes part of our own understanding of wronged human love, a faith view of sin can perceive and speak of a momentary disappointment that somehow stands out in God. This is not far-fetched human projection nor a factor simply flooded away by divine forgiveness. To overlook or even to deny this way that sin affects our lovingly creative God would be to excise the divine gift of sorrow from our hearts. Various Scripture passages point in this direction. In Genesis 6:6 we are told that in the face of the daily wickedness of human beings, "Yahweh regretted having made man on the earth, and his heart grieved." In Isaiah 5:4, God, as the prophet's friend, having labored in the beloved vineyard, puzzles over a disappointing question: "What could I have done for my vineyard that I have not done? I expected it to yield grapes. Why did it yield sour grapes instead?"

This sense of disappointment and the effect of our sin before God are further revealed in the New Testament. In Luke 19:41–44, as Jesus enters Jerusalem for the last time, he sheds tears and reveals a grief that surely speaks more of his disappointment in his beloved people than of any fear for himself. Later, in Luke 22:61–62, Peter's heart is wrung to tears as he encounters, at one and the same time, both the disappointment and the faithful forgiveness in Jesus' eyes. The suffering unto death of Jesus in all his innocence is the effect of our sin before God writ large. These climactic events in Jesus' life are never fully explained. For the believer, they are a mystery and thus inexplicable simply in terms of the history and politics of first-century Palestine. "He died for our sins" is at the core of New Testament theology; the horror of our sins is laid bare and takes its toll before the mystery of God's faithful forgiveness. When the Son of God dies for our sins in reverent obedience, restoration and reconciliation stretch limitlessly throughout the universe, across all history, through all time and space.

Momentary Terror

As sorrow grows and catches fire in the encounter with God's loving forgiveness, another dynamic may well occur. A momentary terror can flare forth in consciousness. In the light of much past unhealthy fear and guilt about sin, one truth becomes extremely important to understand: the terror is not directed at God. Rather, it is a part of God's saving love at work in our hearts and results from two graced insights that pierce the blindness and complacency that often cloud our hearts. First, we see the precariousness of human freedom, placed as it is against the backdrop of the mystery of sin raging in cosmic conflict between good and evil, and finding a focus within every human heart. While originally created in the goodness and beauty of Christ, the whole universe, and each of us, is laced with sin. Our baptism into the dying and rising of Jesus—and therefore, in the Catholic faith, into our substantive goodness in Christ—does not alter or gainsay this doctrine. Second, we may recognize how trapped and helpless we are in the face of such evil; even though our whole purpose is to exist and to have our destiny in God, no willpower of our own can free us from this enslavement.

When these two insights are not simply objects of clear reason but affectively stir the heart with graced clarity, a moment of existential absurdity and contradiction frightens our consciousness. The resonance of this terror within our affectivity is not appealing or pleasant. It is a grace, however, a part of the invitation to greater intimate reliance on, and zealous cooperation with, the mission of loving forgiveness revealed in the mystery of Christ. This grace is no self-scare tactic, though of course it can be mis-used as such. Rather, this fundamental, fearful helplessness in the face of sin and evil, when it is an authentic grace, instructs us of the life-and-death seriousness of our human freedom and of the unquenchable fire of God's love revealed in Jesus crucified. Insofar as this grace is given and received, God's faithful forgiveness is not regarded as cheap or automatic, but is received as a love whose costliness and gratuitousness more and more focus the heart of a repentant sinner on Jesus crucified and so gradually transform fearful helplessness into the humble confidence of a lively reliance.

When we are aware of how radical our reliance on Christ is, the thought of living for a moment outside of Christ is as fear-some as death and hell. For sorrowful sinners, however, Christ on the cross, as the victorious mercy of God, simply bars the gates of hell. For free human beings whose daily lives concern the struggle between good and evil, the hell of life outside of Christ, which is death indeed, remains a possibility that we are blessed to find most fearful. In this graced moment of fright, though the soul may shudder and almost lose its breath, an exhilarating fire for love can be born. It can renew the discovery of the precious, costly gift of human freedom with its permanent consequences of death or life as well as of a God whose faithful love in Christ flames eternally.

A Birthplace of Fire for Ministry

From beginning to end, the central grace motivating and suffusing every stage of this inner journey is the forgiving love of God. This faithful forgiveness is as clear and direct as a much beloved, much loving Son crucified for our sins. The promise this whole journey makes in our hearts is simple and exact: joyous rebirth in the humbling truth of a faithfully forgiving God who is always touched by a contrite heart (Psalm 51:17). This journey, with all its careful moments, roots and renews our very identity in God's loving forgiveness.

This renewed identity brings in its wake a number of other qualities that can reveal and test the genuineness and profundity of a person's journey into God's forgiveness. Generous gratitude, durable joy, and gentle reverence are some of the qualities that typify the forgiven sinner. Aware of being gifted far beyond any personal merit, the forgiven sinner is astonished with gratitude. The steady exuberance of this gratitude must simply overflow in generous love and service, in whatever way God shall desire, among so many needy brothers and sisters. This thankfulness, as profound and precious as a new right to life, is the reversal of sin's insulting ingratitude and becomes the motive for all that is done. It is a gratitude on fire for mission.

The grateful heart, because it is selflessly oriented, always knows profound joy. As born in the heart of a forgiven sinner, this joy is durable, with a steadiness that can weather the storms of serving God's loving justice in our world. The graced remembering of a repentant sinner not only brings exhilarating joy to light the vision of every day but also gives body and a chastened depth to this joy and a discerning, careful quality to apostolic love. This joy is part of the steady flame quickened in the fire of God's forgiveness.

Thankfulness and joy, as great missionary realities, join with gentle reverence in the forgiven heart. The humiliation of forgiveness chastens the soul's sight to recognize our God, beautiful in Jesus, present and at work in all. When such contemplation of reality has been refined in the chastity of a forgiven heart, respectful and gentle reverence is always the fitting, inevitable response. In this way, forgiveness begins to remove the veil that sin imposes on reality, and the gentle reverence of contemplative wonder flames in our hearts until that fullness of time when all vestige of shadow shall be removed and adoring reverence flashes forth in white-hot heat, as our eternal identity in the mystery of a dear God whose forgiving love has been more faithful than we could ever have imagined.

Finally, this graced journey is a birthplace, a place where fire is received and rekindled. It is the fire of the Holy Spirit ready to inflame human hearts that do not resist but let themselves be guided into the mystery of God, aflame with loving forgiveness. This experience of God's forgiveness will not occur—or, if it does, it will be rootless, superficial, and inauthentic—if the stages of the journey described here are rushed or bypassed. All through the experience, careful inner discernment is required. The stages of this journey are meant to be experienced by all believers. The priest, in his own distinctive way, leads the people into this mystery of God in Jesus and calls down the purifying fire of forgiveness for the missionary transformation of our whole universe.

CHAPTER 11

Celibate Chastity: A Priestly Evangelical Imperative

Evangelical Imperatives

Through the documents of Vatican II, the Holy Spirit calls us to a renewal of Christian holiness with a special focus on the universality of God's desire and hope for us all. "Thus it is evident to everyone that all the faithful of Christ of whatever rank or status are called to the fullness of the Christian life and to the perfection of charity."[1] Each person of God is marked for holiness. This marking flames forth in the holy longing that is stirring in all our hearts.[2] A frenzy of desire, like a wildfire in us all, seeks containment and refinement in the fire of God's Holy Spirit of love. This wildfire can glow in quiet incandescence or rage almost beyond control. In either instance, and in every instance in between, such wildfire intimates holiness. The sparks and flames, crackling and humming in our hearts, make hoping for holiness possible for and attractive to us all in the Spirit's fire of love.

This renewed universal call to holiness in the Christian life will brook no false or downgrading divisions. Every disciple is called to the fullness of holiness. Though the life-form of Religious Life has its own professional, single-minded focus on holiness,[3] this does not deny the universality of Christ's call. Each vocation and life-form has its own distinctive spirituality and focus, and nothing less than the fullness of Christian holiness will do for every disciple of the Risen Jesus. Laypeople, diocesan priests, consecrated Religious: all contain and integrate the fire of desire in their hearts in a unique way without downplaying the fullness of life in Christ that God intends.

In his book *A Life of Promise*, Francis Moloney, S.D.B., views chastity, obedience, and poverty as evangelical imperatives. These three virtues radiate and sparkle in the heart and life of the Risen Jesus as revealed both in the Gospels and in our daily experience of his presence. They cut to the heart of who he is. These radical Gospel values bring Jesus close and open us to the vista of God's glorious love for us all, both now and into the fullness of time. As a result, these three Gospel ideals, radiant in the example of Jesus, are more than evangelical counsels that some are invited to embrace. Rather, they form a single integrated ideal that identifies all those baptized into Christ as they seriously follow and intimately serve him. Moloney claims that "the universal vocation to the fullness of the Christian life and to the perfection of love means that all . . . are called to a radical commitment to the values of the Gospel, cost what it may."[4] In *Pastores Dabo Vobis,* John Paul II refers to these same three ideals as the radicalism of the Gospel and claims that "for all Christians without exception, the radicalism of the Gospel represents a fundamental, undeniable demand flowing from the call of Christ to follow and imitate him by virtue of the intimate communion of life with him brought about by the Spirit."[5]

The priest, who shares in the universal priesthood of all the baptized, also roots his life and identity in these three evangelical imperatives. In his role of making Jesus present as Head of the body, the priest is uniquely configured to Christ as head and shepherd, and this configuration calls for his distinctive practice of these evangelical virtues. More than actions done by or imposed on him, they radically situate his heart and soul in the fire of Jesus' heart. They invite and effect an intimacy of union with Jesus in the ministry of shepherding the people. The ultimate orientation of these evangelical imperatives, as for the ministerial priesthood itself, is to call people to a more intimate awareness and enthusiastic living of the universal priesthood that we all share from our baptism together into a whole new vision in Christ. The chastity, obedience, and poverty of the diocesan priest catch fire from the priestly heart of Jesus and radiate a glow of enlightenment for the people whose lives are also shaped in their own way by these evangelical virtues.

These three evangelical imperatives share some similar aspects. First, each of them is motivated by an overwhelming experience of God's love, especially in Jesus crucified into resurrection. Moloney puts it this way: "Swept off our feet by the lordship of a God who is love, we show the world that genuine affection is not found in a predatory man or woman hunt, but in the loss of self, as we are taken over by the presence of so great a love that we can do no other than give ourselves uniquely to that love."[6] Such an overwhelming experience of love lures us out of desire for control. We fall out of control—not irrationally, but irresistibly, gripped by the magnetic appeal of such love. At times, a peak dramatic experience of this love may even have physiological effects: a sudden fire flashes and tingles. At other times the experience is more objectively considered but with the same result: an awareness of genuinely overwhelming love that should not and cannot be resisted. Chastity, obedience, and poverty are each forged in the fire of such an experience and are always about both giving and receiving love.

Second, only the essential integration of all three of these evangelical ideals will stamp a life of love with the integrity of following Jesus Christ. This is no pick-and-choose experience; the full comprehension of each one entails the other two. The life and teaching of Jesus Christ integrate chastity, obedience, and poverty, and we cannot follow him fully without seriously integrating all three into our lives. John Paul II speaks of them as "intimately related."[7] For any baptized disciple, and in a distinctive way for the diocesan priest, following the Jesus of the Gospels will attractively and effectively catch fire only when the three are interrelated; a choice of one or the other never makes sense.

Third, besides being essentially related, each of these virtues is constituted by an important threefold relationship. Chastity, obedience, and poverty each involve a unique personal relationship with God, an appropriate communal web of relationships, and finally, a ministerial impact. To view any one of the imperatives only in light of one or two of these relationships is not only incomplete, but misleading and corruptive of the full meaning of the particular imperative under consideration. In this and in the following two chapters I will touch briefly on all three relationships as we look at the diocesan priest's distinctive practice of each of the evangelical imperatives.

Celibate Chastity

The celibacy of the diocesan priest is much discussed these days. The atmosphere and tone of the discussion often become heated, and even incendiary. The fire can bedazzle and scorch, but it does not always enlighten.

In such a volatile atmosphere it is important to clarify the context of my reflections. Celibacy does not have the same central role and significance in the diocesan priesthood as it does in the life-form of Religious Life.[8] On the other hand, diocesan priestly celibacy is not totally different in its meaning from that of Religious Life. Celibacy has a central core of meaning even though its exact significance will vary in the context of different life-forms or vocational states. In this chapter I am not arguing against the current discipline of celibacy for diocesan priests in the Latin Rite of the Catholic Church. Rather, I want to reflect on the positive meaning and value of celibacy for the diocesan priesthood.[9] It is a way of living that is spiritually and sexually challenging and yet capable of genuine psychological health. The adventure of a healthy celibate life always involves the integration of its sexual challenge with a profoundly intimate, multifaceted spiritual life. My central focus here, however, is not on the sexual dimension of celibacy but on the delicate and decisive balance that priestly celibacy must achieve among the following three essential relationships: a distinctive companionship with God, a life and faith shared appropriately in the presbyteral community, and a ministry shared with many other people.

Toward a Descriptive Definition

As a mystery in faith, celibacy defies any final scientific definition; in fact, it is impossible even to begin to comprehend it without a profoundly personal life of faith. Karl Rahner calls it "part of a theology on its knees, at prayer."[10] He further observes that "it is odd how we always speak of celibacy in general. . . . [T]o take refuge in generalities about such a subject is misguided, dangerous, and self-defeating. . . . You and I must ultimately ask not 'What of celibacy *in itself?*' but 'Where does *my* celibacy stand?'"[11]

My reflections are offered as an invitation to priests to reflect prayerfully on their own experience of celibacy. This is not to say that an individual priest's experience of celibacy is, in itself, definitive of celibacy. Though priestly reflections must be personal and experiential, such reflections must also be kept within the Catholic Christian tradition's understanding of priestly celibacy.

By synthesizing elements of truth from many different statements, I will formulate a description of priestly celibacy that moves from negation to affirmation and from simpler to more refined and careful. For many people (to whom the word itself might be unknown), the celibacy of a priest is a matter of not having a wife. This is true, but an even more precise definition is necessary. Celibacy is the forgoing of all genital sexual expression in the basic fourfold sexual relationship we all have: with members of the opposite sex, with members of the same sex, with ourselves, and with God. Even more subtly and precisely, celibacy also entails the forgoing of romantic behavior, since such behavior gradually becomes more and more seriously oriented to the commitment of marriage. A celibate will not relate to anyone in a way that expresses the seriousness of the romantic. Two quick comments and a reflection on the human experience of celibacy are needed to prevent serious misunderstanding. First, this does not mean that celibacy should deaden a priest's human affectivity so that he never experiences romantic feelings. "Falling in love," with its warm stirrings of romantic feelings, is part of the passionate beauty of human spontaneity. What is called for at this point is an honest acknowledgment of the presence of romantic feelings and

GEORGE A. ASCHENBRENNER, S.J.

a decisive, though not harsh, reorientation of these feelings in a way other than romantic behavior and relationship. Second, in no way does celibacy make friendship with other people something that is suspect or to be avoided. Friendships of all sorts are invaluable gifts that make priestly celibacy possible.

In the human experience of celibacy, the priest does not renounce the totality of human spontaneity. That would be a reckless choice for death and an irresponsible escape from love's exhilarating invitation to life. Though there is a clear affective renunciation involved in celibacy—motivated always by a religious experience, as this chapter makes clear—this is never intended as a renunciation of all affectivity. The celibate's experience is actually quite the contrary. An important confirming sign of a call to celibacy is the love and intimacy of human relationships that expand and stir the heart of a celibate person. A shrunken life of excessive disengagement from love and relationship is not the sign of a healthy celibate commitment. The celibate priest realizes, in the truth of his call, that he could never receive or give more human love and friendship in any other lifestyle. This does not imply a superiority of celibacy over marriage but asserts the validity of this unique person's call. Therefore, within the serious boundaries of celibacy's affective renunciation, rather than viewing love and friendship as suspect obstacles, a priest finds a great richness of human relationship and fulfillment flowering.

Describing celibacy as the negation of specific actions is unsatisfying and fails to catch its attraction and power. No string of clear, correct negations will finally lure and hold a human heart in any vocational context. Only an exciting and beautiful affirmation of love can take our breath away and commit our hearts. Peter van Breeman speaks of the experience of finding oneself "unmarriageable for God's sake."[12] This brings us much closer to the heart of the matter. To be unmarriageable is not seen here as a curse or an immaturity. In fact, a man must first grow to a mature sense of responsibility and marriageablity before the realization gradually dawns that he is actually becoming unmarriageable. Van Breeman puts it well: "Celibacy does not mean that one has lost something, but rather that the celibate has found Someone."[13]

Celibacy, therefore, is the only fitting human response to God's offer of a specific kind of companionship. As a man develops a distinctively intimate and attractive religious life, he feels himself drawn into such an abandonment to this companionship with a dearly loving God in Jesus that he cannot also take upon himself the abandonment and union involved in a marital relationship with another human being. In and through all the loves in his life, he has come upon one Love that transcends and surpasses all the others, and he senses his heart expanding and filling with that Love. This is not to claim that the experience of God found in celibacy is better, more thorough, more intimate, or more holy than that found in marriage, but rather that the celibate priest's experience of God has a different contour and destiny from that of the married person. So understood, celibacy is rooted in a priest's religious experience of the awesome, inviting attractiveness of God's love. The soundings for celibacy must run so clear and deep as to touch the very being and love of God—something too pragmatic and functional will not fan the flame of celibate love. Though there are always many factors contributing to the growth of a priestly vocation, only the infinite beauty of a God who is more in love with us than we are with ourselves can attract a human heart to wholesome celibacy. In the end it is this distinctive companionship with God alone that makes celibacy genuinely religious and makes fidelity to this choice possible.

Essential Threefold Relationship

This brings us to a final description of priestly celibacy as the human faith-presence of someone who lives without a marital partner in response to God's invitation to a distinctive companionship. The distinctive companionship and faith–presence are shared in the community of the presbyterate and of the diocese and radiate for many other people the fire that Jesus knew in his heart from being so loved and cared for at every moment. Priestly celibacy is always more than a matter of overly simple negations; it is not just the performance of certain external actions, not just an inner attitude, not just a private religious experience. Rather, it is a distinctive, human faith-presence lived in the world. This presence is the result of an essential threefold relationship: a distinctive companionship with God, a shared life and faith in the presbyterate and the parish, and finally, a ministry with and for many people.

This threefold relationship is essential. As mentioned earlier, no choice of one or two of the parts will suffice; all three are required and offered in a priestly celibate vocation. We have much yet to learn about this essential interrelationship. We have long been familiar with these three relationships, but we have not always recognized or honored their interdependence. Priestly celibacy can never be fulfilled by something as functional as greater freedom for ministry in the face of the world's needs. For this reason, the traditional phrase "celibacy for the sake of the kingdom of heaven" must be carefully and fully understood.[14] The kingdom is not simply the goal and finality of celibacy. The phrase is meant to express, even more importantly, the present religious experience that calls someone to celibate life and service. It is susceptible to a fuller expression in "celibacy *because of* the kingdom of heaven." In this way Matthew 19:12 reveals Jesus as making himself a eunuch (a celibate) because of his experience, then and there, of a dearly beloved God, of a special reign of love. This "making oneself a eunuch" also furthers that love in our world.[15] The celibate priest stands with Jesus in a similar religious position and must be careful not to downgrade it to a functionalism that will always corrode the gift of celibacy.[16]

The essential threefold relationship with God, presbyterate, and people also proclaims that celibacy cannot be fulfilled only by a special relationship of solitude with God. Excessive individualism has often led to an overly spiritualistic, and therefore deficient, understanding of priestly celibacy. A profoundly personal involvement with God in prayer is absolutely critical for effective celibate living, but such a prayer relationship with God, essential as it is, is not enough.

Within this threefold composite, diocesan priests have the most trouble, as mentioned earlier in this book, with their own appropriate version of an essentially communitarian relationship. It is a problem both of understanding and of practice. Many diocesan priests do not see any special communitarian dimension as part of their vocation, especially among their brother priests in the presbyterate and also, at times, with the people in the parish. This Lone Ranger mentality of diocesan priesthood persists even though such priests are often plagued by painful loneliness. Priests must learn how to acknowledge and appreciate this appropriate sense of community as part of their vocation. Also, within dioceses where this sense of presbyteral and parochial community is recognized as necessary, the engaging in it falls quite short of the mark. These failures in understanding and practice cause both the celibate lifestyle and the whole priestly ministry to suffer. This theme will recur later in this chapter and in the next one, where I discuss the obedience of the diocesan priesthood.

Relationship with God

The most important aspect of this essential threefold relationship is the distinctive companionship initiated by the mysterious workings of God's love in a person's heart—to which, finally, the only appropriate response is a celibate lifestyle and presence. Modern American culture militates against the experience of aloneness in many ways. While he does maintain supportive friendships of all sorts, the celibate priest does in some sense stand alone in this world. The companionship in which this aloneness is rooted is lived in the darkness of faith and in the enthusiasm of hope; there is no regular marital presence, no hand to hold, no eyes to gaze into, no lips to kiss. To stand alone seems freakish in a culture obsessed with the sensual and the sexual, and celibate existence will always be countercultural in the face of such an immature attitude, whether in the secular world or in the church. Though it is true that infatuation with sensual feelings can distract one from the call to profound faith, celibate priests are not bound to scorn and flee the sensual. Rather, they are invited to discover, develop, and live the appropriate expression of their sensuality in relationships with God and with many other people.

GEORGE A. ASCHENBRENNER, S.J.

The aloneness of celibate existence with and in God is a necessary witness to the whole human family, for it symbolizes something fundamental to the human condition. Henri Nouwen has referred to celibacy as "an emptiness for God."[17] At the center of every human heart is a space, an emptiness, available to no one besides that unique human being and God, whose love creatively holds that person in being. This emptiness is truly for God, and this is true for each of us. Mature human and spiritual identity comes from gradually discovering, accepting, and living out of this center. Both celibate and marital lifestyles have their foundation in this core emptiness and aloneness that Nouwen calls "celibate." For this reason, he maintains that "we will never fully understand what it means to be celibate unless we recognize that celibacy is, first of all, an element and even an essential element in the life of all Christians."[18] Celibacy stakes a claim in the heart at a depth that is available only to our creatively loving God. In this way, celibates proclaim that the core identity of us all is radically centered in God. In the soul of each of us quietly burns an eternal white-hot flame.

A Creative Disengagement

Celibate lack of engagement with a spouse announces a profound and intimate engagement in faith with the awesome mystery of a loving God. This disengagement reflects the Calvary disengagement of Jesus, a difficult, deathly disengagement for life, freely chosen as a means to witness unequivocally to his lively engagement with the one he called "my dearly loved Father." His Beloved blessed that disengagement with a fullness of life and love in resurrection. As Sandra Schneiders persuasively argued a number of years ago,[19] the deathly disengagement of Jesus and of the celibate is the creative expression of a kingdom-fullness to be looked for now in hope and to be lived finally in joy. Thus, celibate disengagement not only bespeaks a special engagement with God but also announces to all Christians that their identity, however necessarily and intricately involved it is with this world, is finally not of this world but is fulfilled in that fascinating and mysterious

Beloved of Jesus whose Spirit glows in all our hearts. As Schneiders points out, however, celibacy can be creative only if "such a disengagement, such an engagement with God . . . is completely, authentically, generously, and unselfconsciously lived."[20]

Most authentic, unself-conscious celibate living is born of responsible dealing with loneliness. The uniqueness of each individual person makes loneliness an inescapable part of the human condition, and celibacy is stamped with its own unique potential for loneliness because of its disengagement and affective renunciation. While it has a scorching underside, loneliness also sparks an opportunity for important personal developments, such as a humbly confident self-possession and a richly intimate life with self, with others, and with God. If this loneliness is not properly controlled, however, it tends to fragment us, leaving us with an anguished sense of alienation and a desolation that is destructive of our relationship with our true self, with others, and with God. When celibate loneliness is faced and dealt with, however, it becomes productive and enriching.

Aloneness, the opposite of loneliness, suggests being "all one." It is the centered wholeness of humble self-possession carefully poised for service. Recognizing both the distinction and the relationship between loneliness and aloneness is important to living a celibate lifestyle, but productive dealing with loneliness is more easily described than accomplished. Instead of suffocating in the clutches of loneliness or repressively denying its existence, priests must learn to be present in their loneliness in a way that helps them recognize within the experience itself an invitation to renew their celibate commitment in the intimacy of solitude, alone with God as the Beloved of their hearts. To face the loneliness, to accept it as part of life and yet to avoid being mastered by it through transforming it into a renewal of celibate identity usually involves the use of specific practical tactics that are as varied as the priests who make use of them: a wrestled act of adoration in the flickering light of a chapel, the exuberant exhaustion of physical exercise and hard work, the pleasant enjoyment of music and reading, or the heavenly delight of time with a friend. Whatever tactics are employed, the motivation is the same: to decide to work against the destructive loneliness by finding within its depth the priest's truest self in that quiet white-hot flame that melds all his energies for service.

A Composure of Consciousness

A celibate lifestyle should also involve the development of an imaginative and lively theology and spirituality of "my room" and "my bed." This is quite different from the marital theology and spirituality of "our room" and "our bed." Most people do not usually sit alone in their rooms or go to bed alone. The priest, however, retires alone at night and arises alone in the morning; during waking hours he spends a great deal of time alone in his room either relaxing or preparing for ministry. It is often in the priest's own room and bed that nagging loneliness can tempt his soul and sap his enthusiasm. A theology and spirituality of my room and my bed must be realistic and profound—realistic enough not to delude the priest into thinking that future loneliness can be prevented and profound enough to help the priest transform this ordinary loneliness into a contemplatively relaxed and intimate solitude with God in love.

To be profound and realistic, such a theology and spirituality must be expressed imaginatively and symbolically. Care should be taken, for example, in the priest's arrangement of his room. For something as personal and individual as the decor of a priest's room to succeed as an imaginative and symbolic expression of his theology, it must provide him with a subtle and influential composure of consciousness that reflects and affirms his unique identity in relationship as focused on the fascinating beauty of God in Jesus. The priest's room should not be a fortress protecting him from community or a place for selfish indulgence. It can, however, be a refreshing and encouraging aid to composure of consciousness that focuses the affectivity of his heart so thoroughly in the quiet flame of God's love that he is poised in freedom for service and relationship with anyone, anywhere.

Obviously, this kind of theology and spirituality is not automatically acquired; it must be intentionally developed through hard work over years. The effort, however, can make the difference between a shoddy, sad celibate life and one that is joyous and zealous. The faithful practice of daily contemplation can play a major part in developing this composure of consciousness.

It is now time to look at something else that has been running all through this chapter: the community consciousness appropriate to a diocesan priestly celibate life.

Appropriate Communitarian Sense

As we made clear earlier in this book, the charism of diocesan priesthood is not the same as the charism of consecrated Religious Life. This does not deny that a sense of community is necessary within a presbyterate and in the life of the individual priest. In their treatment of the ministry and life of priests, Vatican II documents make this claim: "Established in the priestly order by ordination, all priests are united among themselves in an intimate sacramental brotherhood."[21] This communitarian bond should not be hampered by the unrealistic expectations of a monastic model in which physical presence plays a central role in the uniting of minds and hearts focused primarily in a faith vision. No, as mentioned earlier in this book, the distinctive spirituality of the diocesan priesthood is active and non-monastic. Therefore, the union of minds and hearts concentrated primarily in a faith vision is not so dependent on physical presence.

The appropriate experience of community among diocesan priests does make a difference; it is not a chimera incapable of realization in a priest's actual experience. Unfortunately, any genuine sense of community among priests within a diocese, deanery, or parish now seems to develop more by personal choice than by any policy, plan, or shared expectation. What is required in many such instances is a whole change of mentality, a different way of conceiving diocesan priesthood that has implications for the way priests are trained in seminaries. An aspect of diocesan priestly reality is presently missing, and the whole picture is out of focus. For example, an effective pastor's perhaps inadvertent attitude that he is lord of the fiefdom of his own parish becomes too narrowly focused and is not supported by or capable of being extended to a diocesan-wide vision. A variety of other attitudes, often contagious in a diocese, will interfere with any community consciousness beyond individual, personal attraction. These interfering attitudes must be recognized, talked about, and changed if a genuine sense of shared vision and mission in companionship is to grow and support *all* the priests in a presbyterate. If this shared vision and mission in companionship become realities, priests who are now living and working alone will feel supported as part of a larger enterprise. This supportive shared vision does not suddenly remove all loneliness and discouragement, but it does provide strength and encouragement, which could not have been otherwise present.

To make this communitarian view a reality, with genuine results in the consciousness of every priest, requires hard work on the part of the bishop, on the part of all the priests, and on the part of programs of priestly formation. In the statement from Vatican II previously cited in this chapter, we read: "In a special way they [all priests] form one presbytery in a diocese to whose service they are committed under their own bishop. For even though priests are assigned to different duties they still carry on one priestly ministry on behalf of men."[22] The council's view is clearly stated, as is that of John Paul II:

> The ordained ministry has a radical "communitarian form" and can only be carried out as a "collective work." The council dealt extensively with this communal aspect of the nature of the priesthood, examining in succession the relationship of the priest with his own bishop, with other priests, and with the lay faithful.[23]

I have two final comments about this essential communal aspect of diocesan priesthood. First, it is crucial that those making the important transition from seminary formation to early priestly ministry have a proper understanding of diocesan priestly community—with realistic, appropriate expectations. Though programs for priestly formation are clear about the communal dimension of seminary life, they do not speak of the cultivation of an important attitude, real and influential, of communal brotherhood beyond the experience of being physically together at Eucharist, Liturgy of the Hours, and other activities. The awareness and practice of a communal presence beyond the physical must be operative when the seminarian moves from the large community of the seminary to a parish ministry, where he is much more physically alone. If this attitude has not been recognized as important, discussed, and cultivated within the training program, then the new priest will have unrealistic expectations and get mired in discouragement and frustration in his early ministry.

Second, the matter of homosexual priests has been addressed in much recent discussion.[24] It is a matter that requires honesty, balance, and great personal concern for all involved, especially those to be served in a diocese. My comments are brief and intentionally placed here as part of my treatment of the communitarian dimension of diocesan priesthood. Claims of percentages of homosexual men in seminaries and in the priesthood have been bruited about. They should not be exaggerated, and in any case, the issue is not chiefly about percentages. The real issue concerns honesty and respect. Personal (not public) honesty about sexual orientation (whether homosexual or heterosexual) is needed, as is respect for each other as united in priestly service, taking care not to get trapped in the exclusive enclave of a subculture. Of course, the signs of a homosexual man's call to celibate diocesan priesthood must reveal, as must that of a heterosexually oriented man, the descriptive elements delineated at the beginning of this chapter.

The development of a detailed subculture, whether gay or straight, that makes the persons of the opposite orientation feel destabilized, doubtful, and excluded should be avoided. Both in seminary and in a diocese this phenomenon of an exclusive subculture is divisive, and therefore it prevents appropriate communal consciousness in the diocesan priesthood.

Though sexual orientation is a matter of personal honesty— and is not always easily interpreted—and though it has genuine social effects that cannot be disregarded, a man's sexual orientation is not the most important issue about him in seminary formation.

GEORGE A. ASCHENBRENNER, S.J.

We should be careful not to overpublicize this issue of sexual orientation into an exaggerated importance, thus blocking more important issues: core, human, and spiritual identity, always the seedbed for the signs of a call to diocesan priestly service of the people. Anything that interferes with the community of a diocesan presbyterate interferes also with the service of the people in the fire of God's love as radiantly promised in Jesus. Much more can be said about this issue. It will challenge us all in honesty, in personal respect for each other, and finally, in our wholehearted commitment to priestly service of the people.

An Essential Relationship to Ministry

To complete this treatment of diocesan priestly celibacy, I must make some reflections about its essential relationship to ministry. The whole structure of my description of celibacy as an essential threefold relationship requires this. Not simply a matter of personal enjoyment or of individual convenience, this ministerial relationship is essential to diocesan priestly celibacy.

Nonetheless, ministry should not assume absolute primacy in the description of celibacy. Without a clear sense of the proper place of ministry, a celibate lifestyle can be confused and corrupted. Without consciously choosing to do so and often without noticing it, diocesan priests can easily identify themselves with their ministry to the extent that it becomes the measure and proof of their worth. What is *done* is very concrete and daily at hand, and thus it is susceptible to this identity transfer. But the priest's identity must radiate from a depth far beyond what he *does*.

Identifying priesthood with ministry rather than in terms of a distinctive spousal companionship with God brings anxiety, confusion, and tension instead of a peace radiated from the quiet flame of Jesus' spousal love relationship with the church. Especially in a time of decreasing numbers, the ideal of active priestly ministry easily becomes too simple and compulsive: be as busy as possible. An ideal of compulsive busyness disrupts the priest's quality of presence among the people. Attitudes of control, domination, and managerial impatience seep into his daily presence, often without his realizing it. When ministry swallows up his whole identity and becomes who he is, then the priest has forfeited the quiet flame of peace for a frenetically flaming wildfire. Without a properly spiritual quality of heart and presence in the events of his busy days, ministry becomes a compulsive flurry that is superficial, unfocused, and far less salvific than it should be.

The ministerial dimension of diocesan priestly celibacy can be overstressed, but if the celibate priest is not creatively and responsibly involved in ministry, he will hardly be capable of fundamental peace and enthusiastic joy. Enthusiastic fire for generation in ministry results from—and is a crucial sign of—healthy priestly celibacy. Without sufficient ministerial orientation, a natural urgency is frustrated and an important expression of the priest's psychosexual energy is missed.

In the ministerial dimension of their lives, priests will form relationships with all sorts of people in a great variety of situations. Acknowledging those types of relationships that violate celibacy can help priests to appreciate even more the clear, inspiring witness that their celibacy is meant to be in all these ministerial relationships. We should not think that genital sexual expression is the only, or even the chief, violation of celibacy. Certain ways of relating, without any hint of genital activity, can also be serious violations of a celibate life. Often what is most insidious about these false ways of relating is that the celibate involved is unaware of their dynamics. As I rehearse some of these relational violations, an honest, conscious focusing on the dynamics is very important.

First, a "bachelor" syndrome has its way of violating celibacy. Bachelors, feeling that the challenge and the vigor of life have passed them by, usually become uninvolved spectators. In self-protection, they often radiate a superior, critical attitude and condescendingly carp at people who are seriously involved with the challenges of life. Undue concern with their own security and hypochondriacal fear for their own health are often further symptoms of this bachelor syndrome. When the celibate commitment slides into a bachelor's style of relating, then a celibacy lived because of the kingdom of God's love is being violated.

GEORGE A. ASCHENBRENNER, S.J.

Second, the workaholic mentality can also provide a frequent escape from the challenge of genuine celibacy. Beyond simple workaholic tendencies, fully developed workaholism is a compulsion for finding as one's chief and most significant satisfaction and challenge an involvement with things rather than with persons, especially in the job done well and completed on time. Workaholics appear externally to be so competent, dedicated, and busy, such juggernauts of activity, that others fear to interrupt them. Internally, and often without their knowing, they do not experience life as a love affair. As a result, they often feel a vague, nagging sadness from which the compulsive work distracts them. This is just the opposite of the fire aglow in the heart of any truly zealous apostle of God's love.

A third violation of genuine celibate relationships is the mentality of clericalism. Because clericalism is based on an unfounded sense of superiority, it involves exaggerated expectations of respect and privilege. Its primary focus is on being served and treated as special, rather than on serving others. In many ways this un-Christlike attitude has been rationalized over the years and has become a systemic evil for which no individual can justifiably be blamed. By violating the basic equality of the whole human family, this clerical mentality often impedes genuine compassion and foments precipitous criticism of things new and different. The bachelor, workaholic, and clerical mentalities (together with other possibilities) violate and limit the effective witness of priestly celibacy. Careful reflection is called for to avoid these unconscious dynamics.

The ministerial relationship also reveals how countercultural priestly celibacy is in this world. A priest who lives a contented, enthusiastic celibate life challenges some strong cultural prejudices without so much as raising his voice. Celibacy proclaims that the meaning of one's identity, being a real man or woman, runs much deeper than the superficial biological proof of genital sexual potency. For this reason, human maturity, whether for an individual or for an interpersonal relationship, does not absolutely require genital activity. Celibacy also announces that the paramount value in human life of a profoundly satisfying joy does not chiefly result from mature genital sexual activity, but from the self-gift of any loving sacrifice. These faith statements about the meaning of human life fly directly in the face of our culture's sexually fixated self-indulgence. To many, such statements seem freakish, impotent, and deranged. Usually they are not even honored with an angry confrontation, but are lightly and casually dismissed with a cynical smile. It takes deep conviction to be able to stand out in the midst of our secular culture. In this situation, both a deep, intimate rootedness in God's love and the support of the presbyteral and parish communities are crucial.

In conclusion, diocesan priestly celibacy as a relationship of distinctive companionship with God essentially requires the two further relationships of appropriate priestly community and ministry. A certain graced facility for mature priestly celibate living arises only from a carefully balanced integration of these three relationships. The final challenge for mature priestly celibate living is to catch the proper balance of this threefold relationship at the various times and seasons of a priest's life. In this way priestly celibacy is an important part of the vocation, a gift given and to be received. Only the careful cooperation of a receptive priest can allow it to bless the church and our world with an enthusiastic human presence that can unleash people's deepest yearnings for a fire of love and joy in God, whose love alone flames eternally and can finally give rest to a restlessly journeying heart.

CHAPTER 12

Diocesan Priestly Obedience:
A Mission in Companionship

In a life of serious Christian discipleship, obedience is another evangelical imperative for all the baptized.[1] The diocesan priest has his own distinctive way of living this imperative, and I will describe that way of living in this chapter. My thesis is that diocesan priestly obedience is in essential relationship with community and mission and is, thereby, productive of a mission in companionship. Stripped of these fundamental relationships, the diocesan priest's obedience is shrunken in a serious misunderstanding.

What I am going to describe is undoubtedly already being practiced in some dioceses to a greater or lesser degree. My claim is that, beyond certain practices in different dioceses, what is needed is an explicitly recognized and consciously articulated new conceptualization of diocesan priestly obedience. Before developing my thesis, I will briefly sketch some different views of obedience in our contemporary secular culture and in the Christian faith of all the baptized. In showing how diocesan obedience is essentially related to unity and apostolic mission, I will describe some fundamental attitudes enjoined on a bishop and his priests—attitudes invited by, and expressed in, a distinctive apostolic placement process. After discussing three concrete signs of the diocesan unity and service produced by this view of priestly obedience, I will briefly sketch the role of the bishop in implementing such a view of diocesan priestly obedience.

The Contemporary Environment

The relationship today between authority and obedience, frequently, even in a faith context, is strained at best and often even nervously distrustful. In such an uneasy alliance, either partner can be a threat to the other in a way that disrupts unity and enervates zeal for service. An authoritarian command to "be quiet and do what you're told" hardly invites mature response and partnership. Nor does the arrogant claim that "nobody's going to tell me what to do" invite responsible dialogue and interaction with religious authority. In recent years the interpretation and practice of obedience and authority have vacillated between these extremes. The reasons for such a tense, vacillating relationship are often obvious.

Further complication in this authority-obedience partnership comes from a persisting development that began a number of years ago. A movement toward decentralization over centralization, toward participative over representative democracy, and toward horizontal networking over vertical hierarchy colors our thinking, feeling, and imagining. The effects of these megatrends on the Catholic Church as a whole, and in most dioceses, since Vatican II are obvious. Although the development of these more participative, decentralizing attitudes at first brought confusion and consternation, it is now clear that in many ways they have enriched and renewed our faith as a church and have enhanced our compassionately decisive involvement in the modern world.

These secular trends and developments, as they continue to enter the bloodstream of believers, also raise some serious questions of identity. What does it mean to be a church? What does it mean to be a diocese? Obviously, the answers to these questions color our view of authority and obedience. The church struggles to recognize the Holy Spirit's invitation to incorporate the influence of certain secular developments while also recognizing "limit" situations in which faith must firmly resist a secular spirit or development. Can the contemporary secular movement toward participative, democratic decentralization finally lead us, as a church, to bury any semblance of hierarchically centralized identity? In my opinion, this challenging question concerns one of those "limit"

GEORGE A. ASCHENBRENNER, S.J.

situations for our Catholic faith. If we are to face the issue honestly and carefully, we must avoid getting trapped in an overly facile either-or assumption about the governing style and organization of any group, whether it is hierarchically centralized or democratically decentralized.

The challenge facing the whole church and every diocese is not to stubbornly reject every sign of participative democracy as corruptive of and contradictory to Catholic hierarchical centralization. Rather, notwithstanding some of the strong secular influence of our American culture, the challenge is to devise a creative and appropriate way to integrate democratic decentralization and hierarchical centralization. This new, creatively integrated model could diminish an alienating sense of fragmentation and increase the sense of membership, involvement, and commitment to mission on the part of all the priests in a particular diocese. This chapter will situate an understanding of the respectful obedience of diocesan priesthood within such a creatively integrated diocesan model.

Aspects of Obedience

Christian obedience is always religiously motivated. Far beyond any purely secular or sociological experience, Christian obedience, and thus diocesan priestly obedience, is always chiefly motivated and determined by the experience of God's love. Johannes Metz pointedly describes the essence of this obedience: "Obedience as an evangelical virtue is the radical and uncalculated surrender of one's life to God the Father who raises up and liberates."[2] As a religious experience, obedience is a priest's response to the entrancing flame of God's love, revealed in the fire of the Holy Spirit radiating in Jesus the High Priest. Without enough genuine knowledge and love of Jesus, the life and service of obedience are deficient, if possible at all. Francis Moloney claims that "Jesus did not found a group of disciples to *control* God's kingdom. He called them to 'follow' him, and to call others to pursue that same journey, to fall, out of control, into the hands of a loving and jealous God, as he leads them into *his* future."[3] The priest's obedience, however anguished or easy, is never a forfeiting of responsible freedom.

Such a life of falling out of control into God is not a heroism of supererogation; rather, it "encompass[es] the whole of the Christian response" and makes obedience "certainly the most radically demanding of all the evangelical imperatives."[4] Once again, without a lively sense of God's love, the priest's life as an obediently faithful response is hardly possible at all. Priestly obedience, as all who practice it know well, demands the flame of a spirituality quickened by the strong wind of lively faith.

Christian obedience to God's love in imitation of Jesus is also always ecclesial. It is mediated within and through the church. Together with acknowledging the inviolability of an individual's maturely and competently formed conscience, it is important to recognize that the obedience of Christian discipleship is not simply an individualistic "God and me" encounter. Ecclesial mediation is central to the fundamental baptismal commitment and continues to play a central role in the obedience of other forms of consecration that further specify and develop that first foundational commitment. It is also the primary community and locus for the formation of conscience.

Though Christian obedience is always finally oriented to an interpersonal experience of God's will of love, the divine authority revealing this will of love is ecclesial and is therefore necessarily mediated in various ways. When these channels of human mediation trouble and challenge us, as they often do, we cannot simply write them off as excessively legalistic minutiae or culturally outdated phenomena. Behind what seems to be simply an outdated governmental style or process of group dynamics may be something much more important: a profoundly theological, spiritual mystery revealed in Christ. That is not disposed of too easily. The human channels of ecclesial authority that mediate God's loving presence will always challenge us to find the proper contemporary mode for its expression, purified enough to symbolize honestly, faithfully, and simply the divine, loving source of all authority.

Because the obedience of Christian discipleship and of diocesan priesthood is always ecclesial and mediated, a solidarity of faith is involved, happening among believers, encouraged by them, and finally deepening their communal unity. This communal dimension of priestly obedience is the focus of this chapter. When seen within the communal context, Christian obedience is, and cannot be anything other than, an interpersonal response to authority. Obedience and authority are so intimately related that it would be a serious mistake to consider the quality of priestly obedience as completely unaffected by the governing style of local episcopal authority. This intimate interrelationship cuts both ways: a childishly unhealthy exercise of authority can invite an immature response of obedience, while only respectful, mature obedience invites and allows an adult, creatively governing authority. The abandonment and submission of self involved in obedience cannot be oblivious to the style in which authority is exercised. A governing style that either allows others to do whatever they want or forces them to do something without any possibility of dialogue and understanding surely affects the quality of obedience. Even more important (and in line with this chapter's central thesis), it affects the unity and zeal of the presbyterate and its service of the people.

Within the Christian community, the relationship of authority and obedience is not that of parent and child. Rather, it is the mature relationship of two or more adults in faith. Whenever a paternalistic interaction of parent and child is substituted for this relationship between peers, the interplay of obedience and authority is corrupted. An overly parental prejudice, especially when combined with a lack of much genuine experience of the expansiveness of God's love, can easily turn the radical entrusting of self in obedience into any one of a whole range of authoritarian dysfunctions. To avoid these problems, a basic attitude of brotherhood among all the priests, with the bishop, is important in a diocese.

Unity for Mission

This brief review of the fundamental mystery of Christian obedience as a religious, ecclesial, and adult experience in which one is always interpersonally related to authority provides a context in which the obedience of a diocesan presbyterate can be viewed as related to communitarian unity and ministry. The evangelical imperative of obedience for the diocesan priest involves the same threefold relationship that is present in priestly celibacy: a uniquely personal experience of God's love in Jesus, a unifying communitarian aspect, and a ministerial dimension. The three relationships are essentially interrelated, and this threefold relationship will be intertwined with my description of diocesan priestly obedience. Mature, serious obedience in a presbyterate will create and promote a deep bond of unity and an enthusiastic service of the people. Without much appropriate priestly community, such mature, serious obedience is hardly possible, and the ministry of service of the people is weakened. In this contemporary age, obedience cannot be thought about, talked about, or practiced without serious acknowledgment of its relationship to diocesan unity and ministry.

In the diocesan priesthood, in contrast to the dynamic at work in a monastic group, an active vision and spirit draw the priests together for the sake of mission; they come together precisely to be sent forth. The physical presence of the priests to each other in community is not the chief identifying characteristic of a presbyterate. It is the desire to be sent forth that attracts the priests from the very beginning. The unity of the presbyterate must never prevent the sending forth of the priests; the presbyterate must find its fulfillment—and its unity too—precisely in that missioning and dispersion.

As a result, although many other characteristics of the priests may and should enrich the group's unity, the most profound and influential bond among them will be rooted in their appropriate sharing of the fire of mission in Jesus. The mission of Jesus is always rooted in the heart of the Trinity, in Jesus' full, intimate, shared life with his Beloved. In the passionate intensity of Jesus' presence and involvement in the world, we recognize the missionary fire of love in the heart of the Trinity that sends him forth. From far beyond the world, Jesus is sent, and as sent, he immerses himself in the joy and sadness, the light and darkness, and all the complicated entanglements of a fully human life. The mission of Jesus, therefore, is much more than the specific work he does. It is, more importantly, an attitude, a mentality that always colors his mission of compassion and his urgent concern for loving justice in this world. This attitude and presence under-

GEORGE A. ASCHENBRENNER, S.J.

lie all that he says and does and is. The Gospel of John makes it especially clear that Jesus comes as one sent and that his mission is rooted in this continual, intimate experience of being sent by the Father. His mission is never a matter of sending himself—there is no hint of self-ignition in the fire in his heart.

> What I have spoken does not come from myself;
> no, what I was to say, what I had to speak,
> was commanded by the Father who sent me,
> and I know that his commands mean eternal life.
> And therefore what the Father has told me
> is what I speak. (John 12:49–50)

> I do nothing of myself:
> what the Father has taught me
> is what I preach;
> he who sent me is with me,
> and has not left me to myself,
> for I always do what pleases him. (John 8:28–9)

It is to this missionary attitude and identity that the Risen Jesus commissions his apostles in the upper room: "As the Father sent me, so am I sending you" (John 20:21). The Acts of the Apostles bears stunning testimony to the corporate availability of the apostles to be sent wherever the Spirit beckoned. The communal identity of the young church seems to have consisted precisely in sharing this apostolic docility to the word of God.

In the active spirituality of a diocesan presbyterate, both bishops and priests must approach sharing the mission of Jesus with an attitude that is similarly attuned and also as practical as the concrete process of apostolic placement. Insofar as an attitude of "being sent as Jesus was" genuinely motivates every member of the presbyterate, and insofar as this is incarnated in the placement process of the diocese, the priestly sharing in the mystery of Jesus' obedience, rather than simply resulting in individual ascetical experiences, can provide a corporate consciousness, a mission in companionship that will fire and unite not only the presbyterate itself but also the whole diocesan church.

Radiating from the bishop to all the priests, this deep-hearted desire to be sent—something clearly contrary both to the trap of sending oneself and to an immature fear of making decisions—requires a humble self-confidence and a continuing experience of the fire of God's missionary love in Jesus. The whole attitude and presence of the bishop and the understanding of the diocesan placement process must invite the prayerful initiative of each priest in an honest, unselfish investigation of God's apostolic will for him here and now. Sometimes God's will is quickly manifested; at other times, it involves anguished soul-searching about selfish prejudices, intense contemplation of Jesus in his passion, and wide consultation with other people. Throughout this initial stage and all the way to the end of the process, the individual priest, while very personally engaged, is never motivated by the attitude or expectation that his own decision about his ministry will be ultimate and self-assertively fixed.

Only a graced freedom can keep each priest seriously engaged in the placement process and ready to receive a ministerial assignment that is not simply his own decision. It is this same freedom that allows a priest's present experience of receiving a diocesan assignment to be a genuine sharing in the mission of Jesus. This freedom will also prevent the same ministry's collapse into a defensively clutched attachment. The freedom needed here is not a passive lack of concern about a future assignment. Rather, it is a dynamic gift created by a strongly intimate experience of God's love and therefore a gift able to inflame an inspiration and energy without which God's apostolic desire might not even be recognized, much less embraced. When necessary, this freedom can even stretch the heart beyond common sense to an agonizing self-abandonment to the glory and fire of God as corporately perceived and corporately served by a presbyterate gathered around its episcopal leader in the challenging, geographically specific range of the diocese.

Apostolic Placement Process

If the sending forth of active apostles is to deepen a unifying bond in Christ and avoid chaos and dissension, then the diocesan religious authority must employ a particular style of government and a particular type of placement process. In this way the apostolic availability and the obedient desire of each priest "to be sent as Jesus was" are invited and afforded concrete expression. Though various adaptations are possible, there must be a fundamental clarity of understanding about the placement process. Otherwise, what was never intended can happen: the process itself can confuse and prevent the desired communitarian experience of obedience.

Part of this process is the expression of an overall apostolic vision and set of priorities in the diocese—not as unilaterally promulgated from on high but, in an appropriate way, as corporately determined within the diocese. In this vision and set of priorities, the unity longed for on the part of the whole presbyterate takes preliminary expression, stirs the Spirit's apostolic inspiration in each priest, and provides a context within which each priest's serious opinion will finally be tested. Whether it is a genuine mission or not will be revealed.

Within a diocese, the role and lines of religious authority must be clear. As a human being and as an ordained minister, each priest has a certain basic authority, but the bishop has a juridical religious authority beyond that of the rest of the priests. If that episcopal authority is truly to render a special service for the corporate unity of the whole diocese, then not only must its presence and role be similarly perceived by all, but it must also function in line with this understanding daily. In this view each priest, through his prayerful engagement in the diocesan apostolic process, receives a specific ministerial assignment that has been decided interpersonally with him and intentionally for him but, finally, not simply by him. The bishop, who has himself been missioned in Christ, always has the final missioning authority in the diocese. This authority cannot be completely delegated to, much less usurped by, a personnel board or any other mechanism in the diocesan structure. I do not mean to downplay the great aid that a personnel board or other diocesan structure can be to communal unity and spirit. Rather, I want to repeat the point that the role and lines of religious authority in the diocese must remain personal as well as clear if they are to be directed toward unity of spirit and mission.

This view of missioning and obedience implies and requires a profound spirituality, something more than sound organizational dynamics and conflict-resolution processes. Often, in the absence of such spirituality, hidden agendas, political maneuvering, and various authoritarian hang-ups creep in and corrupt the experience of obedience. For the individual priest, "being sent as Jesus was" always culminates in an experience of receptivity and mature abandonment of one's whole self—a falling out of control of one's life and into God's providential love, as focused in the ultimate missioning decision of the bishop. Such an entrusting of self is hardly possible unless it is ignited and genuinely inflamed by Jesus' own experience of the glowing fire of a Beloved's faithful love. A lively incarnational faith is needed if one is to recognize and hearken to God's loving call as mediated through the properly exercised episcopal authority of a specific, limited, and duly designated person. This human mediation, expressed in the person of the local Ordinary and eventually grounded in a specific ecclesial understanding, is the quintessence of any incarnational view of diocesan priestly obedience. The main contention of this chapter is that this mediation can also be the chief propellant toward companionship in mission within a diocese.

If a priest makes his own decision about a ministry, with whatever goodwill, or if he manipulates the accomplishment of his own will, even with the apparent legitimation of the placement process, then he does not genuinely participate in or submit to another's decision. Instead, he "sends himself," an event quite opposed to the creative docility of obedience. This sending of self does not just segregate the individual; it splinters the communal energy and zeal of the presbyterate.

The profound spirituality that inspires the diocesan placement process must include a genuine commitment to union in Christ on the part of the bishop and each of his brother priests. Without fostering a misguided, unrealistic sense of familial relationship or religious community, the seminary formation of diocesan priests must encourage a desire for, and some actual experience of, an

GEORGE A. ASCHENBRENNER, S.J.

appropriate communitarian consciousness among the newly ordained. "Loner" and "rugged individualist" attitudes tend not only to disappoint the effectiveness of the individual priest's ministry but also to disrupt a unified diocesan experience of God's loving mission in Jesus. The clear, fresh air of honesty and trust must keep all diocesan channels of communication open.

A genuine concern for a sense of corporate membership and shared mission will make demands on the bishop and all the priests. It will take time and sacrifice and will test the creativity and commitment of all. Occasional, carefully planned gatherings of the whole presbyterate, priest support groups, shared silent retreat experiences of deep solitude, a diocesan newspaper, personal letters and phone calls, and many other means can create a communal sense of priestly companionship and committed membership in the presbyterate. These are not luxuries for leisure time; joyous priestly celibacy demands such bonds of unity. Priestly obedience, when appropriately conceived and lived, can create such a communitarian sense of unity and harness it with an enthusiasm for the generous service of God's people in the diocese.

The Signs of Unity

Unity among the priests in a diocese is something much desired but often not sufficiently worked at because of divergent expectations. Sometimes the unity expected is too superficially uniform in terms of either type of ministry or geographical location. Ministerially, the unity of a diocese can depend too much on whether or not all the priests engage in the same sort of parochial work. Special, exceptional ministries may seem to interfere with presbyteral unity. Geographically, the unity of a presbyterate can depend too much on whether everyone serves within the limited area of the diocese. Although the call to serve a specific people within the boundaries of a diocese is central to diocesan priestly identity, the corporate solidarity of diocesan priesthood should run deeper than geography and should not be disrupted by occasional necessary ministry outside the diocese. Although they surely have some effect on priestly unity, ministerial uniformity and geographical proximity cannot provide the deepest foundation for the corporate identity of a diocesan presbyterate.

The creative docility of priestly obedience, as expressed in the shared attitude of "being sent as Jesus was" through the proper diocesan apostolic placement process, can lay a much more dependable foundation for unity and mission, rooted in the experience and heart of each priest in the presbyterate. Enthusiastic and unified service to all the people of a diocese demands much more than an uncertain unity superficially based on ministerial uniformity and geographical proximity. The people themselves expect more, and the priests' promise before God of respect and obedience to the bishop makes them capable of a more effective communal identity for mission.

The profoundly corporate and missionary identity of the diocesan priesthood can manifest itself in at least three ways. First, obedient unity in the experience of "being sent" produces a special consciousness of solidarity. Each priest knows that he has been missioned to a specific ministry in a specific place in order to share with his brother priests in Jesus' mission from his Father. It has not simply been a matter of his own choice. To speak of administering a parish that "belongs to the whole diocese" is no cute or pious use of words; it delineates a clear mentality of corporate stewardship. Such an attitude, so different from the possessive one that clings to "my parish," conceives of every ministry as rooted in the Trinity and mediated through Jesus Christ and the bishop. When these become simply grandiose, high-sounding words, quite removed from the daily mentality and experience of the priests of a diocese, they then bespeak a serious failing in faith and a defective priestly obedience. If each priest's apostolic assignment is genuinely seen as rooted in the heart of the Trinity and mediated through Jesus Christ and episcopal authority, it therefore somehow belongs to the presbyterate as a whole, and each priest will find his heart strengthened and encouraged by a communal bond of solidarity and shared membership that stretches far beyond the physical presence of his brother priests. In the growing phenomenon of one-priest parishes, this encouraging bond of solidarity is nothing less than a lifeline.

GEORGE A. ASCHENBRENNER, S.J.

Second, a corporate understanding of priestly obedience makes possible another important realization, that in some real way, all the different diocesan priestly ministries are of equal importance. Surely, in some ways, not all diocesan priestly ministries are of completely equal importance. Yet if each ministerial assignment—from bishop's secretary to resident in the retired priest's home to pastor of a sprawling inter-city parish—is genuinely perceived as a particular brother priest's share in Jesus' mission in the Spirit from his Father, then there can be a basic and profound respect for all these ministries. Far from being an ethereal, vague distinction, this realization of the basic equality of all diocesan ministries is great protection against some very real attitudes that we commonly adopt, such as, and especially, competitive and ambitious attitudes that destroy diocesan unity. These attitudes of ambitious jealousy and competitive rivalry can be avoided if communitarian priestly obedience reveals in some way the equal value of all diocesan assignments as genuine participation in the radiant fire of Jesus' own mission. Whatever the circumstances—whether one is assigned to a full-time position as a hospital chaplain, to be the pastor of an affluent suburban parish, or to be an assistant pastor of a financially insecure parish ambitious attitudes will not be provoked in such an atmosphere of communitarian priestly obedience.

Third, the consciousness of priestly solidarity effected by shared obedience is also the best antidote, and perhaps the only effective one, to the kind of criticism that can divide a diocese—especially criticism of new and experimental ministries. If the few priests engaged in these new ministries know themselves to have been chosen and sent as Jesus was, and are so known by other priests of the diocese, then in some real way these special ministries belong to the whole diocese, to the whole presbyterate, and are not the possessions of the individual priests involved. Rather than disgruntled criticism or prideful possessiveness of these special ministries, what is needed is the persevering support of prayer and priestly interest, especially since new and experimental ministries often involve unique loneliness and challenge.

Role of the Bishop

Having described the process of priestly obedience, I will now briefly sketch the role of the person who has a special religious authority in the process, in this case, the diocesan bishop. First, it should be clear to all that he too is a man of obedience, following the leading of God's Holy Spirit in his heart as carefully as he can. The possession of religious authority does not excuse him from practicing obedience; in many ways, in fact, it intensifies his sensitivity in obedience.

In line with the central point of this chapter, religious authority is a gifted service for unity and mission within the presbyterate and in the diocese as a whole. The threefold relationship involved in priestly obedience is so essential that it prevents us from even conceiving of obedience outside of that integrated vision of a unique personal relationship with Jesus as shepherd, a bond of solidarity with the whole presbyterate, and a ministry of service of the people in the diocese.

In the midst of this vision of priestly obedience, the bishop, because of his gift of special religious authority, plays a distinctive role. This role must always serve the unity of the presbyterate, of the whole diocese, and of the universal church. I will describe two models of the bishop's role that catch extremes at each end of the spectrum and thus do not accomplish the goal of his special service.

First, a "control" model is possible, in which the role of the bishop is to keep everything under control. The role of everyone else is to "fit in" as expected. This model turns the episcopal office into more of a cross than it is meant to be. Its excessive concern and overextended control siphon off the bishop's energy and can gradually destroy even the most competent of men. It tends to enforce uniformity rather than a healthy charismatic unity.

Second, a "permissive" model is possible. In this model, the role of the bishop is to "let be," to let affairs run their own course and basically to stay out of the priests' way. At first, this down-playing of authority is very popular, but over time, a growing confusion, a lack of vision in the diocese, and a lack of felt unified membership on the part of the priests surface in lassitude and

GEORGE A. ASCHENBRENNER, S.J.

discontent. If simply allowed to run their own course, diocesan events will not serve a healthy communal unity in the presbyterate or a unified service of the people in the diocese. To achieve a mission in companionship in the presbyterate and in the whole diocese, a different model is needed.

Once the inadequacy of these two models is recognized, the proper role of the bishop in the communal search for and service of God's will of love in the diocese can be appreciated. He is the spiritual leader and focal point of the unified living of priestly identity, both ministerially within the presbyterate and universally among the people. Though administrative gifts are essential to this role, they do not have a primacy of importance. As spiritual leader, the bishop does not have to be recognized publicly as the holiest person of all. He knows his weaknesses and he struggles to abandon his heart to God, as we all do. From his central position as overseer of the whole diocese, however, he is a channel of communication for the presbyterate. He organizes things so that no part of the diocese feels left out or uninformed. He has a special role in quickening the fire of God's love throughout the whole diocese.

Finally, in this service of special authority he inspires and invites self-disclosure among all the priests. Not simply a matter of friendship, this self-disclosure makes possible among brother priests a genuine accountability regarding the authentic unified living of priestly identity in the diocese. In an appropriate way, the priests are—and want to be—their brothers' keepers. This disclosure is not easy for most priests. It challenges their self-protective, secretive styles. Nonetheless, the challenge is not only worth the risk but must be addressed if a presbyterate and diocese really desire the shared flame of companionship in mission. This invitation for self-disclosure and shared accountability is part of the bishop's central involvement in the missioning process described earlier.

Each bishop must clearly understand the role presented here and then develop a structure that allows him to fulfill this role in his own unique way. The role I have described allows for considerable adaptation as long as the central focus of presbyteral obedience for the sake of unity and mission in the diocese is not lost. This role can never leave everything up to the bishop. He can never accomplish, by himself, the daily development of unity and ministry. A basic fraternal relationship among the priests, with the bishop and with the people, focused in a genuine desire on the part of all for union in and service of the fire of love radiating in Jesus the High Priest—this dynamic, when it suffuses a diocese, makes possible the whole approach described here.

Obedience Is a Shared Mystery

In this chapter I have presented a conceptualization—perhaps somewhat new—of the obedience of the diocesan priesthood as promised before God to the bishop. I have described an apostolic placement process and a style of government that call forth and incarnate on the part of every priest in a diocese the shared mentality of "being sent as Jesus was." In this view, obedience within a diocese becomes much more than a set of regulations or an empty protocol. Rather, as a profound mystery shared in faith, obedience becomes a life, a vision, and a mission binding priests and bishop together as servant members in the midst of the whole people united for evangelization.

I suspect that in some cases, any acceptance of this chapter's suggestions may involve a challenging conversion of attitude and process—perhaps more than I can personally appreciate from outside the ordinary diocesan framework. However, my admiration and respect for the diocesan priesthood give me the conviction that we are well capable of, and could be deeply helped by, what I suggest here. Insofar as these suggestions become reality, I believe that the promise and practice of obedience will create a profound unity of priestly brotherhood, a brotherhood at once gathered around the bishop and decisively focused in joyful, magnanimous service to God's people. All priests feel the need for the fellowship of priestly brotherhood, and wise ones seek it as best they can. We have also learned in recent years that this can misfire into either an exclusivist clericalism or an unhealthy "men's club" mentality. Or such bonding can be utterly nonexistent.

GEORGE A. ASCHENBRENNER, S.J.

If we reconceive the implications of the promise of respect and obedience made on ordination day, then the fellowship of priestly brotherhood, besides involving enjoyable social times together, will be rooted in a shared religious experience of Calvary, where a faithful Son, as High Priest, has fallen out of control and into the loving hands of a dear Father—a Son who then, as now, in resurrection, knows and reveals an eternal fire of love in the Spirit, a mission in companionship.

Gospel Simplicity

The third evangelical imperative is poverty, or as we will suggest just below, gospel simplicity. I will describe some of the implications of this gospel virtue for the diocesan priesthood.

Introductory Clarifications

This topic is prone to much confusion and misunderstanding. Often discussions about the issue produce, in strong feelings and opinions, a lot of heat but little light. Karl Rahner's comment about celibacy in chapter 11 applies here.[1] Though some general elements and orientations of poverty and simplicity in Christian discipleship are needed, this complex issue is finally a matter of *my* lifestyle. To avoid some confusion right from the start, I offer some introductory comments.

First and foremost, a matter of terminology must be faced. Sandra Schneiders claimed in 1986 that the primary analogue for the word *poverty* is something economic and sociological.[2] In this sense, poverty signifies an economic state of not having what one needs to live a good human life. It describes an unjust economic insufficiency. Therefore, it is an evil, an economic condition that we should work hard to abolish. The word has a very different meaning when considered as an evangelical imperative. In this usage, poverty refers to a vision and lifestyle motivated explicitly by a religious experience. It is intimately and immediately related to the fire of God's love radiant in the example of Jesus and aflame in our human hearts. Without enough personal experience of this radiantly satisfying love, a priest either would never give a second thought to the choice of a simple lifestyle or might fix on such a style for a variety of nonreligious reasons, such as upbringing, convenience, fiscal necessity, or personal irresponsibility. In such an apparently simple lifestyle, the finger of God is not present. The word *poverty* is still used with this religious significance in the Christian tradition, as witness Vatican II, *Pastores Dabo Vobis,* and a large number of spiritual writers. I am not recommending a complete change of terminology here, but I will interchange *poverty* and *gospel simplicity* in this chapter.

As a gospel value, this simplicity cannot be forced or legislated. No coercion is acceptable. Simplicity is a value and a virtue that radiates from the heart of God and glows on the face of Jesus the High Priest. Serious contemplation of Jesus can inflame our hearts as this ideal catches fire for us. John Paul II puts it this way: "In reality, only the person who contemplates and lives the mystery of God as the one and supreme good, as the true and definitive treasure, can understand and practice poverty."[3] We speak here of a profound mystery in faith; without lively, prayerful faith we just cannot appreciate such a value. In fact, we will probably come up with intelligent arguments in opposition.

Though the simplicity described here has as its primary analogue an ongoing religious experience of God's loving-kindness, such as we see in Jesus' experience in the Gospels, this poverty cannot be oblivious to or unrelated to the shockingly real economic poverty that plagues so many of our human brothers and sisters. We become narrowly unrealistic when our spiritually motivated simplicity is somehow hermetically sealed off and protected from the hard facts of the economic injustices in our world. Gospel simplicity has as a passionate part of its religious motivation a disquiet, even an outrage, at the harsh, unjust economic inequalities in our world. In our excessively consumeristic society, products and merchandise assume such major importance ahead of people that such products shrink and suffocate our identity. In such a situation, simplicity can seem harsh, austere, and even inhuman. In a world so topsy-turvy, gospel simplicity puts us on the side of the economically disadvantaged and sets us against the flagrant flaunting of economic power and riches. The warmth and beauty of any situation depends much more on the presence of kindly, hospitable people than on lavish decor.

I want to make one final introductory caution. Ordination to the priesthood is explicit about promises of celibacy and obedience. No such explicit promise is made about poverty or gospel simplicity. As previously described,[4] the ineluctable interrelationship of the three evangelical imperatives however, brings this simplicity along, not as an unwelcome intruder but as an essential constituent of the fire burning in the heart of Jesus the High Priest and glowing on his face.

The rest of this chapter will propose a number of distinctions and dimensions of a gospel simplicity that always enhances the witness of diocesan priesthood. Though such gospel simplicity also challenges his personal faith, it ignites and kindles a whole-hearted union of the individual priest with Jesus and, not to be forgotten, also forges a unity of all the priests of a presbyterate in the same fire of Jesus' High Priestly love. The vision presented here invites each priest to serious prayer, reflection, and discussion to help him find the spirit and the details of lifestyle to which the Holy Spirit is now calling him and his brother priests.

The Importance of a Vision of Gospel Simplicity

At one point, Vatican II spoke of the need "to be poor in both fact and spirit, and have . . . treasure in heaven."[5] Only a combination of spirit and factual results, of vision and concrete lifestyle, gives gospel simplicity any hope of developing and perduring in a diocesan priest's life and ministry. It is easy to wax eloquent about the theory and vision of gospel simplicity, but such theory remains disincarnate until the vision bites into one's lifestyle. At the same time, to rush the task of decisively carving out the details of a simple lifestyle in advance of enough experience of the fire of God's love is doomed to double failure: it will not radiate a witness that is truly Christian, and it will not perdure. Being poor in spirit as well as in fact is the essential integration that will structure the remainder of my reflections.

GEORGE A. ASCHENBRENNER, S.J.

The vision of a simplicity of heart revealed in Jesus is written in the ontological state of human existence. A fundamental poverty of dependence on God anchors human existence at its core. Although we find it hard to face in these days when autonomous self-sufficiency is idolized, we do not belong to ourselves, and we are not completely in charge of our existence. Something as frail as a solitary breath reveals this reality and mystery. Each breath is a priceless gift given to us. We are not in total control of our breathing; an existential poverty exists at the core of our person. The experience of a fragile, minuscule, and yet absolutely important breath is beyond our willpower and links us beyond ourselves to a Creator on whom we are utterly dependent. This is no enforced slavery. It reveals human life as the precious gift of a loving Creator right through to the last breath, which lasts, literally, forever. A basic, existential dependence defies the arrogance of total human control, like a wall that withstands the banging of many heads. When properly perceived, this dependence blesses us in a breath-by-breath intimacy and immediacy with a Creator who is awesomely close and loving. The quality of the experience depends on our own view of and response to the reality of our existence.

Implied in the previous description is another way of stating the truth of human existence. Paul reminds the believers in Corinth, "What do you have that was not given to you?" (1 Corinthians 4:7). This has been shorthanded to the simple statement "All is gift." Such an all-encompassing view of human life and of all reality seems too good to be true. Once again, our graced ability to recognize it and respond makes all the difference. Since a gift is never something we deserve or have a right to, full giftedness becomes possible for us only insofar as we can embrace our core vulnerability in the concrete daily attitude that we deserve nothing. This is no posture of depressing self-rejection and condemnation. This posture of radical poverty and foundational openness welcomes the blessing of loving the gift in everything. Not just what we like and prefer, but absolutely everything reveals the faithful love of our Creator. This attitude of deserving nothing touches the very taproot of our existence. The utter reality of being is a gift given to and to be received by each of us. Before God, none of us has a right or a claim on being, nor the means to effect our coming to be. Absolutely everything else—basic human rights of life, liberty, and the pursuit of happiness—depends on that first gift, that sheer gift of being. To deserve nothing is an attitude that cuts across the grain of the predominant secular views of our postmodern society, but only insofar as we can trustingly embrace our profound existential vulnerability are we blessed and gifted beyond imagining.

Gospel simplicity is based in the existential poverty of our utter dependence on a loving Creator. The priest who has not faced or is not able to accept the existential poverty of his being will never be able to initiate a simple lifestyle with enough rooted-ness to perdure in witnessing to God's love in Jesus. Without a lively sense of this vision and spirit of poverty, no factual lifestyle of simplicity is possible. The mechanics of a simple lifestyle must be rooted in a God-given simplicity of heart.

The foundation for gospel simplicity leads us beyond any ideological preference and into the depths of simplicity and poverty in the heart of God. In a startling fashion, poverty in the heart of God is revealed in the mystery of Jesus' experience on Calvary. In "Good News to the Poor,"[6] a chapter from his book *Dilemmas of Modern Religious Life,* J.-M. R. Tillard, O.P., says: "God's preference for the poor goes beyond His willingness to open up for them the ways of justice. Its nature is fully revealed in the mystery of Jesus. And here we are at the very heart of the Gospel."[7]

Tillard claims that

> God's choice of the poor is so complete and absolute that he does not limit himself to being God-for-the-poor or even God-with-the-poor, but in Jesus God-was-made-poor. . . . Jesus is God *made* poor, because on His Cross (and culminating in the Resurrection, which set the seal on His belonging to the mystery of God), He made the condition of mankind in its most tragic aspects His own."[8]

Calvary reveals a poor man—not a rich, selfish man—at the center of salvation. The disgraced, humiliating emptiness of Jesus on

Calvary reveals God as poor and saving for us all. This Poor Man, rejected, scorned, stripped even of the felt experience of being Son, lets his life fall out of control, and it falls into the faithful hands of a Beloved whose loving intimacy has been present in faith all along. For it is in the very moment of such a horrendously poor dying that this faithfully trusting Son is blessed with the most precious gift—a fullness of life in resurrection. Jesus' experience of breathing his last on Calvary proclaims the utter sufficiency of his Beloved's love: "Your love is better than life itself" (Psalm 63:3).

Jesus' dying on Calvary, transcending any limited economic and sociological meaning, is an experience of dire poverty in which—if one can go deep enough in faith to find love within the real horror of Calvary's experience—Jesus is most attractive and glistening with promise. Once again, this hearkens back to the monasticism of the heart described in chapter 3, which bears repeating. Without a continually developing experience of this heartfelt monasticism, nothing described in this book will be possible for the priest, including this vision and spirit of gospel simplicity. Gospel simplicity can never be sufficiently motivated by causes—even good, valuable causes—of our contemporary historical world, such as an ideological position of whatever stripe, a plan to correct economic injustices, a personal health concern. No, gospel simplicity as a vision and a spirit stretches to the length of God. To sound its depths is to experience a fire of love radiating in the heart of God, even in disgrace, humiliation, emptiness, and falling out of control.

Factual Simplicity of Lifestyle

The specifics of an honestly simple lifestyle always presume as a foundation enough experience of the vision and spirit of gospel simplicity just described. Otherwise, the lifestyle is short-circuited and fails. The seed of such a spirit yearns for planting in the soil of a concrete lifestyle, but usually some experience of the vision and spirit comes first. Many years ago, Ladislas Orsy, S.J., stated it this way: "Unless one is rich in God and with God, one cannot be poor in this world."[9] Simplicity must be concrete if it is to be real.

It usually involves giving up things, good things, creatures of God, for love. By sacrificing these things our hearts rely more immediately, more directly, more existentially on God for the nourishment and fulfillment of love. What should I give up, when should I give up, and how much should I give up are questions open to many legitimate influences and answers. To keep our imaginative reflection concrete as this chapter proceeds, examples of what could be involved are decor of a residence, availability of time, and the style of any number of things, such as food, dress, car, or recreation. Honestly discerning one's way through these concrete possibilities must always be an experience of grace and the richness of God's love. For the rest of this chapter I will make some further suggestions to lure the graced imagination and desire of priests to follow the Holy Spirit in seeding the soil of their own lifestyles.

An important distinction sets the stage for what follows. Within the church, two different types of vocation characterize the integration and blending that every disciple of Jesus must discern, that of the vision and spirit of gospel simplicity with the factual details of a simple lifestyle. The first type involves the gifted awareness that the factual details of a seriously simple lifestyle compose the very identity of the person or of the group. In the second type, the person or group is identified differently, according to availability, mobility, flexibility of mission, and active ministry. The diocesan priesthood as a vocation fits into this second group. In the first type, the heart is enraptured by the beauty of a full-hearted trust in God's faithful love as written, for all to read, in the serious simplicity of a lifestyle, and the attractiveness and exuberance of such trust identifies the person or group. This is a specially challenging and beautiful vocation. The discernment of the specifics of the lifestyle is fairly fixed and does not fluctuate much because the lifestyle is the very identity of its members. Such identity is not to be compromised. For these people, a seriously simple lifestyle is who they are, and who they are, in simplicity, *is* their mission. Thus, adaptation for greater ministerial effectiveness is not the issue. Some examples might be Francis and Clare of Assisi, the Missionaries of Charity, and the Little Brothers and Sisters of Jesus, to mention just a few.

In the second type, identity focuses on a flexibility for active mission. Therefore, the specifics of a simple lifestyle will be determined by the specifics of the ministry and cannot be settled before entry into the ministerial situation. In a group of this type, a variety of ministries will produce a variety of legitimate expressions of a simple gospel lifestyle. Without enough freedom both for ministerial flexibility and for appreciation of the basic dynamics of this type, a hardened rigidity and critical misjudgment can choke the life out of healthy availability and unity in a presbyterate. There will be and there should be a variety of simple lifestyles. The priest ministering in the poor inner-city parish will not be clerically attired in exactly the same style as the priest attending a fund-raising dinner for the chief benefactors in the diocese. The discernment of lifestyle in this second type is not as simple and straightforward as is that of the first type. Here, fitting the simple gospel lifestyle to the ministry will first require an entry into the ministerial situation, then a continuing desire to share Jesus' own Calvary reliance on his Beloved, and finally an honest sorting out of the mixture of inner spirits. The honest, loving challenge of a friend or a spiritual director can provide invaluable help in clarifying this discernment.

To ignore or confuse this basic distinction of the dynamics of God's grace regarding gospel simplicity in the church leads to a misunderstanding that is disruptive of the unity and ministry of a presbyterate. The question can arise of whether a diocesan priest can be given a call that identifies him in the specifics of a seriously simple lifestyle. This is surely possible and can be a grace for the priest himself and for the whole presbyterate and diocese. Such a grace will flourish only with humility and a lack of self-righteous misjudgment on the part of the priest himself and with a loving sense of appreciation of the dynamics sketched here on the part of the whole presbyterate and diocese.

Solidarity with the Economically Poor

For most priests, to honestly discern the graced simple lifestyle appropriate for them will require ongoing reflection and sensitization. In our contemporary, excessively consumer-oriented culture, the sacrifice expressed in the priest's lifestyle puts him where he belongs, on the side of the economically poor. Such solidarity with the poor is open to many valid expressions, but it will quickly lose its heart without any reflective experience of the economically poor. Such experience can put a human face on the motivation required for a priest to assess his heart and make whatever adjustments are needed for a simplicity of lifestyle that will radiate the gospel value of God's love, that treasure beyond price, as it continues to shine on the face of Jesus the High Priest. Another part of the priest's discernment of the appropriate simple lifestyle begins in seminary training with a serious investigation of, and readiness to change when needed, his natural tastes in food, dress, and possessions. Finally, a bumper sticker I recently saw catches our point here: "Live simply so others can simply live!"

A lack of sensitivity to the poor can throw the witness of our whole life out of focus. In a brief essay written more than thirty years ago, Charles Davis wrote of the kind of confirmation that the witness of a celibate life needs through voluntary poverty.[10] Without the confirming witness of a simple lifestyle, a celibate life does not resonate with God's reign of love but proclaims a fear of sex, something perhaps far removed from the celibate's intention, but, in an oversexed culture, insidiously countermanding that intended witness. The renunciation in celibacy must be confirmed in a gospel simplicity if the priest's life is to radiate God's love and promise in Jesus. "A comfortable bachelordom is no sign of the Kingdom."[11] An insensitivity in the priest's heart because of lack of solidarity with the poor will often dim his witness beyond what he is aware of or intends.

Simple Lifestyle and Presbyteral Community

Gospel simplicity in lifestyle should not be reduced for a diocesan priest to a private personal devotion. The witness of a whole presbyterate of priests is far greater than the sum of its parts. Not only does such a communitarian witness provide needed support

GEORGE A. ASCHENBRENNER, S.J.

for each priest, but its loud, clear word becomes a ministry in itself throughout the diocese. How sad it is when an individual priest finds that the most insidious temptation to his own struggle for a simple lifestyle comes from his brother priests, often shrouded in a humor that thinly conceals ridicule. I mean to condemn no one here. Some of this temptation is built into the human dynamics of a social gathering. I do want to invite diocesan priests—and all of us—to the mutual support and joy of a simple lifestyle that can open another level of our hearts to, and can radiate for others, a fire of love beyond anything we could enkindle on our own.

Bearing in mind the earlier description of diocesan priesthood as identified not in the specifics of a serious simple lifestyle itself but in a fluidity for mission, priests will need to appreciate the legitimacy of a variety of simple lifestyles and the mystery of human weakness that marks us all. It is precisely because of such weakness that priests—like all of us—need the support, encouragement, and challenge of others as they discern the specifics of their priestly call. Though the fact of a simple lifestyle involves daily concrete specifics, our human makeup is such that these external details either can be waylaid by profound inner attitudes or, more to be desired, can be a public sign that a deep inner attitude has been transformed. Possessiveness, as an attitude, is the contrary of simplicity. This attitude will always gainsay and waylay any attempted simple lifestyle. A presbyterate of priests possessed by the fire of the Holy Spirit in service of the people will have burned away a lot of that possessiveness that deforms us all, and such a presbyterate will issue a loud countercultural call that speaks of the power of a radiant reliance on God's all-sufficing love in Jesus.

Simple Lifestyle and Work

Poor people must work hard each day just to live. For this reason, issues of minimum wage and employment opportunities are never minor. The hard, dedicated work of the priest for his people, his pastoral charity, flows from the gospel simplicity of his heart and his lifestyle. To live supported by others, like landed gentry, would destroy any witness of a simple lifestyle to God's love for us all. As someone who knows he is not his own and so lives fully dedicated to God's service of the people, the priest in his daily hard work demonstrates the generosity and "survival" quality of the poor.

In this relationship of simple lifestyle to work, another distinction assumes importance for the active priest. In his ministry, the priest may have to deal with the finances for comfortable buildings, high-tech equipment, and other parish needs. It is easy for the economics of such situations to rub off on his personal lifestyle. In such a pastoral setting, not only should his personal lifestyle reveal a gospel simplicity different from the economics of his ministerial involvement, but the simplicity of lifestyle should also provide the firepower and wisdom to inspire such involvement of the priest on behalf of his people.

A simplicity of lifestyle based on the gospel witness of Jesus is in many ways inconvenient and uncomfortable. Strange how we can experiment at times for a convenient way to witness gospel simplicity! The inevitable inconvenience of a simple lifestyle is a sacrifice, a suffering that provides grist for the grace of ever more generous service. This inconvenience can have a ministerial limit for the class of people whose identity is mobility for mission. When the inconvenience of a personal lifestyle of simplicity interferes with mobility for ministry, then ministry is chosen over lifestyle preference because for members of this class, ministerial mobility cuts more deeply into the priestly identity. However, this distinction, true though it is, will require serious reflection lest it loosen into a loophole for rationalization. Ministry can easily be misused to rationalize away any inconvenience in a simple lifestyle. The freedom and docility that come from the Holy Spirit can protect us from these rationalizations. Vatican II speaks to this issue in its own way: "From this freedom and docility will grow a spiritual discernment through which a proper relationship to the world and its goods will be worked out. Such a relationship is highly important for priests, since the church's mission is fulfilled in the midst of the world."[12]

GEORGE A. ASCHENBRENNER, S.J.

Conclusion

It would be incorrect to see poverty and gospel simplicity as the ultimate value in the Christian vision. In the light of Jesus, who reveals the heart of God, the ultimate value, beyond all others, is love. Even Francis and Clare of Assisi, whose names are almost synonymous with gospel simplicity and poverty, make this very clear. Their entire lives were about love, and simplicity and poverty were a means to that grace. Sometimes an all-encompassing concern for poverty brings in its wake an unloving stinginess, competitiveness, and judgmentalism. In this case the limpid water of simplicity and poverty has been stirred to a foul cloudiness. In 1 Corinthians 13, Paul states the unassailable truth: "[W]ithout love . . . I am nothing at all. . . . [T]he greatest . . . is love" (vv. 2, 13).

When an appropriate lifestyle of gospel simplicity is aflame in a priest's life, it can hone his soul to a keen insight and wisdom for loving. In these days of continuing polarization in the world and in the church, gospel simplicity can enlighten the way for the patient, loving work of bridge building. This is one of the most needed ministries in the church now, but it can have a special importance for the diocesan priest as he serves right in the midst of those polarizing tendencies that inhabit all our hearts.[13]

Br. David Stendl-Rast once suggested a simple and challenging approach to receiving the grace of gospel simplicity. Once we have sorted out our needs and our wants, he claimed, we must respect, and cannot tamper with, our needs. We can, however, probe our wants. "To want less and less is to thank more and more."[14] The thankfulness of a priest loved beyond any measure ignites the fire of gospel simplicity.

Mary of Nazareth, in her life and her Magnificat, knew the wisdom, intimacy, and fire of such simplicity and gratitude. They are the song and signature of her very identity. She had learned early to want less and less, so the eye of her heart had a simplicity and a gratitude that kept her lifestyle radiantly uncluttered and always quickening her one great desire, for Jesus.

Conclusion

The scandalous particularity of God's desire fixes each of us in a gaze of love. Conceived in divine love, we are the apple of God's eye, now and into eternal life. The blessing of this original promise in Christ will never be forsaken. Such a blessing invites response. In fact, the final outcome of life depends on our response, whether it is full hearted, complacently dull, or angrily denied. God's own desire in Jesus, however, is clear and contagious: that each of us respond in love's full abandon. Focused in the particularity of that loving gaze and previewed in that response of abandonment is a whole distinctive spirituality that is meant to become the very life of each of us. This unique response entices us into relationship with God in Jesus, thereby fusing us together as necessary members of the whole Body of Christ in our world.

The thesis and development of this book build on a conviction about the particularity of God's love. That particularity fleshes out a distinctive spirituality for the diocesan priesthood, a spirituality that partially overlaps with other vocations but that, in its fullness, is true and fitting for diocesan priests, and for them alone. This point seems especially important today.

After describing the integration of an active, non-monastic lifestyle with a profound core experience of intimacy alone in God's love, I etched in three chapters of charisms a multifaceted picture of diocesan priesthood. That picture identifies a priest as someone chosen, sensitized, and specially empowered to call down fire, the fire of God's creative love. In the radiance and heat of that fire, the priest doctors the souls of others, who often are seeking for what they do not know and cannot name. Carefully and confidently guiding people into that mysterious fire and quickening its flame in our midst—this is the heart and soul of diocesan priesthood.

Since priests are not born fully formed, I described in two chapters some of the implications of this priestly spirituality for a seminary formation program. Central to this formation process is a radical reorientation of person that calls for and develops a presence—more than a ritual of actions—that glistens in our midst with many different gifts: discernment, forgiveness, celibacy, obedience, simplicity. It is a radiant presence, not inertly comatose but active, concentrating laserlike on the fire of God's love, forging together a whole presbyterate and quickening that flame of love in the hearts and souls of us all. Beyond seminary, an important ongoing formation requires that the priest's own soul continue to be doctored, nourished, and shaped as he allows himself to be guided into the mystery of fire and love in Jesus.

This noble, challenging spirituality and ministry are always ignited and flamed in the heart of Jesus the High Priest: "I have come to bring fire to the earth, and how I wish it were blazing already!" (Luke 12:49).

Notes

INTRODUCTION

1. In this introduction I am using with permission some material previously published in "Gold Purified in the Fire: Diocesan Seminary Formation," *Seminary Journal* (winter 1997).

2. See Donald B. Cozzens, *The Changing Face of the Priesthood* (Collegeville, Minn.: Liturgical Press, 2000).

3. Rev. Stephen J. Rossetti, "Priesthood in Transition," *Human Development* (summer 2000): 30.

4. Francis Dorff, O. Praem., "Are We Killing Our Priests?" *America* (April 29, 2000): 7–8.

5. Thomas Keating, *Open Mind, Open Heart* (New York: Continuum, 1992), 3.

6. Walker Percy, *Signposts in a Strange Land* (New York: Farrar, Straus and Giroux, 1992), 316–18.

CHAPTER 1

1. Though "Reflections on the Morale of Priests," published by the Bishops' Committee on Priestly Life and Ministry of the National Conference of Catholic Bishops, addressed the morale issue in March 1988, few would agree that the issue has been resolved.

2. Msgr. Cornelius M. McRae, "Toward a Spirituality of the Diocesan Priesthood," *Seminary Journal* (fall 1999): 32.

3. Robert Barron, "How to Build a Better Priest," *US Catholic* (December 1997): 10–16.

4. Pierre Teilhard de Chardin, "The Mass on the World," in *Hymn of the Universe* (New York: Harper and Row, 1965), 21.

5. See Robert Barron, "How to Build a Better Priest," 11. Also see Robert Barron, "Mystagogues, World-Transformers, and Interpreters of Tongues: A Reflection on Collaborative Ministry in the Church," *Seminary Journal* (summer 1994): 10–13.

CHAPTER 2

1. George Aschenbrenner, "Active and Monastic: Two Apostolic Lifestyles," *Review for Religious* (September 1986): 653–68.

2. In my reflections on the monastic ideal I have in mind groups such as the Carthusians and Cistercians.

3. Galatians 5:22–3.

CHAPTER 3

1. I am well aware of the potential for the word *monasticism* to be misunderstood by some diocesan priests. *Monasticism of heart,* as used here, is carefully distinguished from, and yet essential to rooting, the monastic lifestyle. In a different terminology, it is very similar to the experience of *purity of heart,* which is fundamental to traditional Christian spirituality. However, I choose the phrase *monasticism of heart* in the hope that it catches better both the profundity of heart involved and the contrast intended to the monastic lifestyle.

2. In this chapter I am using with permission material previously published in George Aschenbrenner, "Monasticism of the Heart: The Core of All Christian Lifestyles," *Review for Religious* (July 1990): 483–98.

3. See Kenneth Leech, *True God* (London: Sheldon Press, 1985), 142ff.

4. See Karl Rahner, "Ignatian Mysticism of Joy in the World," in *Theological Investigations,* vol. 3 (Baltimore: Helicon, 1967), 281–3.

5. See George Aschenbrenner, S.J., "Consciousness Examen," *Review for Religious* (January 1972): 14–21; "A Check on Our Availability: The Examen," *Review for Religious* (May 1980): 321–4; and "Consciousness Examen: Becoming God's Heart for the World," *Review for Religious* (November 1988): 801–10. Some of this material is reproduced with permission in the appendix of this book.

6. See Henri Nouwen, *The Road to Daybreak* (New York: Doubleday, 1988), 81–2, for a treatment of the distinction between what is urgent and what is important.

7. See Henri Nouwen, *The Way of the Heart* (New York: Seabury, 1981), 19–40.

8. See John 14:23 (NRSV): "Those who love me will keep my word, and my Father will love them, and we will come to them and make our home with them."

CHAPTER 4

1. Carl J. Arico and M. Basil Pennington, O.C.S.O., *Living Our Priesthood Today* (Huntington, Ind.: Our Sunday Visitor, 1987), 34.

2. Paul Keyes, *Pastoral Presence and the Diocesan Priest* (Whitinsville, Mass.: Affirmation Books, 1978), 16–18.

3. Ibid., 17.

4. Ibid., 18.

5. Ibid., 48.

6. John Paul II, *Pastores Dabo Vobis* (Boston: St. Paul Books and Media, 1992), 44, #23.

7. As will be explained in the first couple of pages of chapter 13, I am interchanging *poverty* and *gospel simplicity* throughout the book.

8. John Paul II, *Pastores Dabo Vobis,* 41, #21.

9. "Dogmatic Constitution on the Church," in *The Documents of Vatican II* (New York: America Press, 1966), 27, #10.

10. Cardinal Roger Mahony and the Priests of the Archdiocese of Los Angeles, *As I Have Done for You* (Chicago: Liturgy Training Publications, 2000), 26.

11. Ibid., 28.

12. Ibid., 26.

13. John Paul II, *Pastores Dabo Vobis,* 43, #22.

14. Ibid.

15. Ibid., 43–4, #22.

16. "Decree on the Ministry and Life of Priests," in *The Documents of Vatican II* (New York: America Press, 1966), 549, #7.

17. Bishop Matthew Clark, "The Relationship of Bishop and Priest," *Origins* (November 9, 2000): 351–6.

18. "Decree on the Ministry and Life of Priests," 547, #7.

19. Walter Burghardt, S.J., *Long Have I Loved You* (Maryknoll, N.Y.: Orbis, 2000), 243.

CHAPTER 5

1. See Karl Rahner, *Servants of the Lord* (New York: Herder and Herder, 1968), 169.

2. Gisbert Greshake, *The Meaning of Christian Priesthood* (Dublin: Four Courts Press, 1988), 156–7.

3. See George Aschenbrenner, S.J., "Becoming Whom We Contemplate," *The Way Supplement* (spring 1985): 30–42.

4. Avery Dulles, S.J., *The Priestly Office* (New York: Paulist, 1997), 18, referring to Karl Rahner, "Priest and Poet," in *Theological Investigations,* vol. 3 (Baltimore: Helicon, 1967), 313.

5. Walter Burghart, S.J., *Long Have I Loved You* (Maryknoll, N.Y.: Orbis, 2000), 127–9.

6. Ibid., 128.

CHAPTER 6

1. See chapter 2, 7–15.

2. Mark O'Keefe, O.S.B., *In Persona Christi: Reflections on Priestly Identity and Holiness* (St. Meinrad, Ind.: Abbey Press, 1998), 32.

CHAPTER 7

1. In this chapter I am using with permission some material previously published in "Gold Purified in the Fire: Diocesan Seminary Formation," *Seminary Journal* (winter 1997).

2. See Edward Pfnausch, "The Conciliar Documents and the 1983 Code," in *The Spirituality of the Diocesan Priest,* ed. Donald Cozzens (Collegeville, Minn.: Liturgical Press, 1997), 156–72.

3. See Philip J. Murnion, "Leadership for a Missionary Community," *Seminary Journal* (fall 2000).

4. Henri Nouwen, *The Way of the Heart* (New York: Seabury, 1981), 19–40.

5. See Murnion, "Leadership for a Missionary Community," 16.

6. Henri Nouwen, *Clowning in Rome* (New York: Image Books, 1979), 13, 21–2.

7. Ibid., 87–108.

8. Murnion, "Leadership for a Missionary Community," 19.

9. See chapter 4, 27–40.

10. John Paul II, *Pastores Dabo Vobis* (Boston: St. Paul Books and Media, 1992), 41–6, #21–#23.

CHAPTER 8

1. In this chapter I have slightly revised, with permission, what was previously published as "Presumption for Perseverance and Permanence: Rudder for Direction and Balance in Priestly Formation," *Seminary Journal* (spring 1988).

2. See chapter 7, 60–67.

CHAPTER 9

1. See George Aschenbrenner, S.J., "A Hidden Self Grown Strong," in *Handbook of Spirituality for Ministers,* ed. Robert J. Wicks (New York: Paulist, 1995), 228–48.

2. Ibid., 236–40.

CHAPTER 10

1. See George Aschenbrenner, S.J., "The Inner Journey of Forgiveness," *Human Development* (fall 1989): 15–23. In this chapter I am using with permission material adapted from this article.

CHAPTER 11

1. "Dogmatic Constitution on the Church," in *The Documents of Vatican II* (New York: America Press, 1966), 67, #40.

2. Ronald Rolheiser, *The Holy Longing* (New York: Doubleday, 1999).

3. See Sandra M. Schneiders, I.H.M., *Finding the Treasure* (New York: Paulist, 2000), 126–37.

4. Francis Moloney, S.D.B., *A Life of Promise* (Wilmington, Md.: Michael Glazier, Inc., 1984), 15.

5. John Paul II, *Pastores Dabo Vobis,* (Boston: St. Paul Books and Media, 1992), 53, #27.

6. Moloney, *A Life of Promise,* 111–12.

7. John Paul II, *Pastores Dabo Vobis,* 53, #27.

8. See Schneiders, *Finding the Treasure,* 54–61.

9. In this chapter I am adapting with permission two previously published articles: "A Celibate's Relationship with God," *Human Development* (winter 1984): 38–43; and "Celibacy in Community and Ministry," *Human Development* (spring 1985): 27–35.

10. Karl Rahner, *Servants of the Lord* (New York: Herder and Herder, 1968), 167.

11. Ibid., 160.

12. See Peter van Breeman, *Called by Name* (Denville, N.J.: Dimension, 1976), 241–52.

13. Ibid., 245.

14. See Moloney, *A Life of Promise,* 103–8.

15. See Raniero Cantalamessa, O.F.M. Cap., *Virginity* (New York: Alba House, 1995), 3–12.

16. See William P. Sheridan, "Functionalism Undermining Priesthood," *Human Development* (fall 1999): 12–6.

17. Henri Nouwen, *Clowning in Rome* (New York: Image Books, 1979), 45ff.

18. Ibid., 45.

19. See Sandra M. Schneiders, I.H.M., "Celibacy: Creative Disengagement," *Sisters Today* (December 1969): 191–200.

20. Ibid., 200.

21. "Decree on the Ministry and Life of Priests," in *The Documents of Vatican II* (New York: America Press, 1966), 549, #8.

22. Ibid.

23. John Paul II, *Pastores Dabo Vobis,* 35, #17.

24. Two examples would be Donald Cozzens, "Facing the Crisis in the Priesthood"; and James Martin, S.J., "The Church and the Homosexual Priest," both in *America* (November 4, 2000): 7–10 and 11–15.

CHAPTER 12

1. In this chapter I am adapting with permission material that was previously published as "The Diocesan Priest's Obedience," *Human Development* (summer 1989): 32–8.

2. Johannes Metz, *Followers of Christ* (New York: Paulist, 1978), 67.

3. Francis Moloney, S.D.B., *A Life of Promise* (Wilmington, Md.: Michael Glazier, Inc., 1984), 160–1.

4. Ibid., 119.

1. See Karl Rahner, *Servants of the Lord* (New York: Herder and Herder, 1968), 160.

2. See Sandra M. Schneiders, I.H.M., *New Wineskins* (New York: Paulist, 1986), 169–70.

3. John Paul II, *Pastores Dabo Vobis* (Boston: St. Paul Books and Media, 1992), 57, #30.

4. See chapter 11, p. 108.

5. "Decree on the Appropriate Renewal of Religious Life," in *The Documents of Vatican II* (New York: America Press, 1966), 475, #13.

6. J.-M. R. Tillard, O.P., *Dilemmas of Modern Religious Life* (Wilmington, Md.: Michael Glazier, Inc., 1984), 60–84.

7. Ibid., 67.

8. Ibid., 68.

9. Ladislas M. Orsy, S.J., *Open to the Spirit* (Washington: Corpus Books, 1968), 110.

10. See Charles Davis, "Empty and Poor for Christ," *America* (October 8, 1966): 419–20.

11. Ibid., 420.

12. "Decree on the Ministry and Life of Priests," *The Documents of Vatican II*, 567, #17.

13. See George Aschenbrenner, S.J., "Quiet Polarization Endangering the Church," *Human Development* (fall 1986): 16–26.

14. From a talk by Br. David Steindl-Rast.

Appendix

In this appendix I am reprinting with permission a slightly amended, updated version of three previously published articles about consciousness examen. Though I have not given it a full separate treatment in the book, its importance in living a serious Christian spirituality is obvious. This type of daily examen helps the priest to monitor the fire of the Spirit in his own soul and then to tend and quicken that fire in the midst of us all.

"Consciousness Examen"

Examen is a practice without much significance for many people in their spiritual lives. This is true for a variety of reasons, but all the reasons amount to the admission (rarely explicit) that it is not of immediate practical value in a busy day. My point in this article is that all these reasons and their false conclusion spring from a basic misunderstanding of this spiritual practice. Examen must be seen in relationship to discernment of spirits. It is a daily intensive exercise of discernment in a person's life.

Examen of Consciousness

For many people today, life is spontaneity if anything. If spontaneity is crushed or aborted, then life itself is stillborn. In this view, examen is living life backwards and once removed from the vibrant spontaneity and immediacy of the experience itself. These people today disagree with Socrates' claim that the unexamined life is not worth living. For these people, the Spirit is in the spontaneous and so anything that militates against spontaneity is not of the Spirit.

This view overlooks the fact that welling up in the consciousness and experience of each of us are two spontaneities, one good and for God, another evil and not for God. These two types of spontaneous urges and movements happen to all of us. So often, the quick-witted, loose-tongued person who can be so entertaining and the center of attention and who is always characterized as being so spontaneous is certainly not being moved by or giving expression to the good spontaneity. For people eager to love God with their whole being, the challenge is not simply to let the spontaneous happen but rather to be able to sift through these various spontaneous urges and give full existential ratification to those spontaneous feelings that are from and for God. We do this by allowing the truly Spirited spontaneity to happen in our daily lives. But we must learn the feel of this true Spirited spontaneity. Examen has a central role in this learning.

When examen is related to discernment, it becomes examen of *consciousness* rather than of conscience. Examen of conscience has narrow moralistic overtones. Its prime concern was with the good or bad actions we had done each day. In discernment, the prime concern is not with the morality of good or bad actions; rather, the concern is with the way God is affecting and moving us (often quite spontaneously!) deep in our own affective consciousness. What is happening in our consciousness is prior to and more important than our actions, which can be delineated as juridically good or evil. How we are experiencing the "drawing" of God (John 6:44) in our own existential consciousness and how our sinful nature is quietly tempting us and luring us away from intimacy with God in the subtle dispositions of our consciousness—this is what the daily examen is concerned with prior to a concern for our response in our *actions*. Hence, it is examen of consciousness that we are concerned with here, so that we can cooperate with and let happen that beautiful spontaneity in our hearts that is the touch of God and the urging of the Spirit.

Examen and Spiritual Identity

The examen we are talking about here is not a Ben Franklin–like striving for self-perfection. We are talking about an experience in faith of growing sensitivity to the unique, intimately special ways that God's Spirit has of approaching and calling us. Obviously, it takes time for this growth. But in this sense, examen is a daily renewal of and growth in our spiritual identity as unique flesh-spirit persons loved and called by God in the inner intimacy of our affective world. It is not possible for us to make an examen without confronting our own unique identity in imitation of Christ before God.

And yet so often our daily examen becomes so general and vague that our unique spiritual identity does not seem to make any difference. Examen assumes real value when it becomes a daily experience of confrontation and renewal of our unique spiritual identity and an experience of how God is subtly inviting us to deepen and develop this identity. We should make our examen each time with as precise a grasp as we have now on our spiritual identity. We do not make it as just any Christian but as this specific Christian person with a unique vocation and grace in faith.

Examen and Prayer

The examen is a time of prayer. The dangers of an empty self-reflection or an unhealthy self-centered introspection are very real. On the other hand, a lack of effort at examen and the approach of living according to what comes naturally keep us quite superficial and insensitive to the subtle and profound ways of God deep in our hearts. The prayerful quality and effectiveness of the examen itself depend upon its relationship to our continuing contemplative prayer. Without this relationship, examen slips to the level of self-reflection for self-perfection, if it perdures at all.

In daily contemplative prayer, God carefully reveals to us the order of the mystery of all reality in Christ—as Paul says to the Colossians: "God has planned to give a vision of the full wonder and splendor of the secret plan for the nations" (Colossians 1:27). The contemplator experiences in many subtle, chiefly nonverbal ways this revelation of God in Christ. The presence of the Spirit of the risen Jesus in the heart of the believer makes it possible to sense and "hear" this challenge to order ourselves to this revelation. Contemplation is empty without this "ordering" response.

This kind of reverent, docile (the "obedience of faith" Paul speaks of in Romans 16:26), and nonmoralistic ordering is the work of the daily examen—to sense and recognize those interior invitations of God that guide and deepen this ordering from day to day and not to cooperate with those subtle insinuations opposed to that ordering. Without that contemplative contact with God's revelation of reality in Christ, both in formal prayer and in informal prayerfulness, the daily practice of examen becomes empty; it shrivels up and dies. Without this "listening" to the revelation of God's ways, which are so different from our own (Isaiah 55:8–9), examen again becomes that shaping up of ourselves that is human and natural self-perfection, or, even worse, it can corrupt into a selfish ordering of ourselves to our own ways.

Examen without regular contemplation is futile. A failure at regular contemplation emaciates the beautifully rich experience of responsible ordering to which the contemplative is continually invited by God. It is true, on the other hand, that contemplation without regular examen becomes compartmentalized, superficial, and stunted in our lives. The time of formal prayer can become a very sacrosanct period in our day but so isolated from the rest of our life that we are not prayerful (finding God in all things) at that level where we really live. The examen gives our daily contemplative experience of God real bite into all our daily living; it is an important means to finding God in everything and not just in the time of formal prayer, as I will explain at the end of this article.

A Discerning Vision of Heart

When we first learn and practice the examen, it seems stylized and artificial. This problem is not in the examen-prayer but in ourselves; we are beginners and have not yet worked out that integration in ourselves of a process of personal discernment to be expressed in daily examens. As beginners, before we have achieved much of a personalized integration, an exercise or process can be very valuable and yet seem formal and stylized. This should not put us off. It will be the inevitable experience for the beginner and for the "old-timer" who is beginning again at examen.

But examen will always be fundamentally misunderstood if the goal of this exercise is not grasped. The specific exercise of examen is ultimately aimed at developing a heart with a discerning vision to be active not only for one or two quarter-hour periods in a day but continually. This is a gift from God—a most important one, as Solomon realized (1 Kings 3:9–12). So we must constantly pray for this gift, but we must also be receptive to its development within our hearts. A daily practice of examen is essential to this development.

Hence the five steps of this exercise of examen as presented in the *Spiritual Exercises* of St. Ignatius Loyola (#43) are to be seen, and gradually experienced in faith, as dimensions of the Christian consciousness, formed by God's work in the heart as it confronts and grows within this world and all of reality. If we allow God gradually to transform our minds and hearts into that of Jesus, so that we become truly Christian through our living experience in this world, then the examen, with its separate elements now seen as integrated dimensions of our own consciousness looking out on the world, is much more organic to our outlook and will seem much less contrived. So there is no ideal length of time arbitrarily set for each of the five elements of the examen when it is practiced. Rather, the examen is a daily organic expression of the spiritual mood of our hearts. At one time we are drawn to one element longer than the others and at another time to another element over the others.

The mature Ignatius, near the end of his life, was always examining every movement and inclination of his heart, which means he was *discerning* the congruence of everything with his true Christ-centered self. This was the overflow of those regular intensive prayer-exercises of examen every day. As beginners or "old-timers" we must understand both the point of the one or two quarter-hour exercises of examen each day—namely, a continually discerning heart—and the point of the necessary gradual adaptation of our practice of examen to our stage of development and to the situation in the world in which we now find ourselves. And yet we are all aware of the subtle rationalization of giving up formal examen each day because we have "arrived at" that continually discerning heart. This kind of rationalization will prevent further growth in faith sensitivity to the ways of the Holy Spirit in our daily lives.

Let us now take a look at the format of the examen as presented by St. Ignatius in the *Spiritual Exercises,* #43, but in light of these previous comments on examen as discerning consciousness within the world.

Prayer for Enlightenment

In the *Exercises,* Ignatius has an act of thanksgiving as the first part of the examen. The first two parts could be interchanged without too much difference. In fact, I would suggest the prayer for enlightenment as a fitting introduction to the examen.

The examen is not simply a matter of the natural power of our memory and analysis to go back over a part of the day. It is a matter of Spirit-guided insight into our lives and courageously responsive sensitivity to God's call in our hearts. What we are seeking here is that gradually growing appreciative insight into the mystery that I am. Without God's revealing grace this kind of insight is not possible. We must be careful not to get locked into the world of our own human natural powers. Our technological world poses a special danger in this regard. Founded on a deep appreciation of the inter-personal, the Christian in faith transcends the boundaries of the here and now with its limited natural causality and discovers a God who loves and works in and through and beyond all. For this rea-son, we begin the examen with an explicit petition for that enlight-enment that will occur in and through our own powers but that our own natural powers could never accomplish all by themselves: that the Spirit may help us to see ourselves a bit more as God sees us!

Reflective Thanksgiving

Our stance as Christians in the midst of the world is that of poor persons possessing nothing, not even ourselves, and yet being gifted at every instant in and through everything. When we become too affluently involved with ourselves and deny our inherent poverty, then we lose the gifts and either begin to make demands for what we think we deserve (often leading to angry frustration) or blandly take for granted *all* that comes our way. Only the truly poor person can appreciate the slightest gift and feel genuine gratitude. The more deeply we live in faith, the more we become aware of how poor we are and how gifted; life itself becomes humble, joyful thanksgiving. This should gradually become an element of our abiding consciousness.

After the introductory prayer for enlightenment our hearts should rest in genuine faith-filled gratitude to God for the personal gifts of this most recent part of our day. Perhaps in the spontaneity of the happening we were not aware of the gift and now in this exercise of reflective prayer we see the events in a very different perspective. Our sudden gratitude—now the act of a humble, selfless pauper—helps make us ready to discover the gift more clearly in a future spontaneity. Our gratitude should center on the concrete, uniquely personal gifts that each of us is blessed with, whether large and obviously important or tiny and apparently insignificant. There is much in our lives that we take for granted; gradually God will lead us to a deep realization that *all is gift*. It is only right to give praise and thanks!

Practical Survey of Actions

In this third element of the examen, ordinarily we rush to review, in some specific detail, our actions of that part of the day just finished so we can catalog them as good or bad. Just what we shouldn't do! Our prime concern here in faith is with what has been happening to and in us since the last examen. The operative questions are what has been happening in us, how has God been working in us, and what is being asked of us? And only secondarily are our own actions to be considered. This part of the examen presumes that we have become sensitive to our interior feelings, moods, and slightest urgings and that we are not frightened by them but have learned to take them very seriously. It is here in the depths of our affectivity, at times so spontaneous and strong and at other times so shadowy, that God moves us and deals with us most intimately. These interior moods, feelings, urges, and movements are the "spirits" that must be sifted through, discerned, so we can recognize God's call to us at this intimate core of our being. As we have said above, the examen is a chief means to this discerning of our interior consciousness.

This presumes a real faith approach to life—that life is first listening, then acting in response. The fundamental attitude of the believer is of one who listens. It is to the Lord's utterances

GEORGE A. ASCHENBRENNER, S.J.

that he gives ear. In as many different ways and on as many varied levels as the listener can discern the word and will of the Lord manifested to him, he must respond with all the Pauline "obedience of faith." It is the attitude of receptivity, passivity, and poverty of one who is always in need, radically dependent, conscious of his creaturehood.[1]

Hence the great need for interior quiet, peace, and passionate receptivity that attunes us to listening to God's word at every instant and in every situation and *then* to responding in our own activity. Again, in a world that is founded more on activity (becoming activism), productivity, and efficiency (whereas efficacy is a norm for the kingdom of God), this faith view is implicitly, if not explicitly, challenged at every turn in the road.

And so our first concern here is with these subtle, intimate, affective ways in which God has been dealing with us during these past few hours. Perhaps we did not recognize God's calling in that past moment, but now our vision is clear and direct. Secondarily, our concern is with our actions insofar as they were *responses* to the calling of the Holy Spirit. So often our activity becomes primary to us, and all sense of response in our activity is lost. We become self-moved and self-motivated rather than moved and motivated by the Spirit (Romans 8:14). This is a subtle lack of faith and a failure to live as a son or daughter of God. In the light of faith, it is the *quality* of responsiveness of the activity, more than the activity itself, that makes the difference for the kingdom of God.

In this general review, there is no strain to reproduce every second since the last examen; rather our concern is with specific details and incidents as they reveal patterns and bring some clarity and insight. This brings us to a consideration of what Ignatius calls the particular examen.

This element of the examen, perhaps more than any other, has been misunderstood. It has often become an effort to divide and conquer by moving down the list of vices or up the list of virtues in a mechanically planned approach to self-perfection. A certain amount of time was spent on one vice or virtue, and then we moved on to the next one on the list. Rather than a practical, programmed approach to perfection, the particular examen is meant to be a reverently honest, personal meeting with the Holy Spirit of God in our own hearts.

When we become sensitive and serious enough about loving God, we begin to realize that some changes must be made. We are deficient in so many areas, and so many defects must be done away with. But God does not want all of them to be handled at once. Usually there is one area of our hearts where God is especially calling for conversion, which is always the beginning of new life. God is interiorly nudging us in one area and reminding us that if we are really serious about life in the Spirit, this one aspect of ourselves must be changed. This is often precisely the one area we want to forget and (maybe) work on later. We do not want to let God's word condemn us in this one area and so we try to forget it and distract ourselves by working on some other, safer area that *does* require conversion but not with the same urgent sting of consciousness that is true of the former area. It is in this first area of our hearts, if we will be honest and open with God, that we will very personally experience the fire of the Holy Spirit confronting us here and now. So often we fail to recognize this guilt for what it really is or we try to blunt it by working hard on something else that we may want to correct, whereas God wants something else here and now. For beginners, it takes time to become interiorly sensitive to God before they gradually come to recognize the Spirit's call to conversion (maybe involving a very painful struggle) in some area of their lives. It is better for beginners to take this time to learn what God wants their particular examen now to be rather than just to take some assigned imperfection and get started on it.

And so the particular examen is very personal, honest, and at times a very subtle experience of the Spirit calling in our hearts for deeper conversion. The matter of the conversion may remain the same for a long period of time, but the important thing is our sense of this personal challenge to us. Often this experience of God's calling for conversion in one small part of our hearts takes the expression of good, healthy guilt that should be carefully interpreted and responded to if there is to be progress in holiness.

When the particular examen is seen as this personal experience of God's love for us, then we can understand why St. Ignatius suggests that we turn our whole consciousness to this experience of the Holy Spirit (whatever it may be in all practicality, for example, more subtle humility, or readiness to get involved with people on their terms, etc.) at those two very important moments in our day, when we begin our day and when we close it, besides the formal examen times.

In this third dimension of the formal examen, the growing faith sense of our sinfulness is central. This is more of a spiritual faith reality as revealed by God in our experience than a heavily moralistic and guilt-laden reality. A deep sense of sinfulness depends on our growth in faith and is a dynamic realization that always ends in thanksgiving—the song of a "saved sinner." In the second chapter of his book *Growth in the Spirit,* Francois Roustang speaks very profoundly about sinfulness and thanksgiving. This can provide enormous insight into the relationship of these second and third elements of the formal examen, especially as dimensions of our abiding Christian consciousness.

Contrition and Sorrow

The Christian heart is always a heart in song—a song of deep joy and gratitude. But the Alleluia can be quite superficial and without body and depth unless it is genuinely touched with sorrow. This is our song as sinners constantly aware of being prey to our sinful tendencies and yet being converted into the newness that is guaranteed in the victory of Jesus Christ. Hence, we never grow out of a sense of wonderful sorrow in the presence of our Savior.

This basic dimension of our heart's vision, which God desires to deepen in us as we are converted from sin, is here applied to the specifics of our actions since the last examen, especially insofar as they were selfishly inadequate *responses* to God's work in our hearts. This sorrow will especially spring from the lack of honesty and courage in responding to God's call in the particular examen. This contrition and sorrow is neither a shame nor a depression at our weakness but a faith experience as we grow in our realization of our dear God's awesome desire that we love with every ounce of our being.

After this description, the value of pausing each day in formal examen and giving concrete expression to this abiding sense of sorrow in our hearts should be quite obvious and should flow naturally from the third element of practical survey of our actions.

Hopeful Resolution for the Future

This final element of the formal daily examen grows naturally out of the previous elements. The organic development leads us to face the future, which is now rising to encounter us and become integrated into our lives. In the light of our present discernment of the immediate past, how do we look to the future? Are we discouraged or despondent or fearful about the future? If this is the atmosphere of our hearts now, we must wonder why and try to interpret this atmosphere; we must be honest in acknowledging our feelings for the future and not repress them by hoping they will go away.

The precise expression of this final element will be determined by the organic flow of this precise examen now. Accordingly, this element of resolution for the immediate future will never happen the same way each time. If it did happen in the same expression each time, it would be a sure sign that we were not really entering into the previous four elements of the examen.

At this point in the examen there should be a great desire to face the future with renewed vision and sensitivity as we pray both to recognize even more the subtle ways in which God will greet us and to recognize the Spirit calling us in the existential situation of the future and then to respond to that call with more faith, humility, and courage. This should be especially true of that intimate, abiding experience of the particular examen. Great hope should be the atmosphere of our hearts at this point—hope not founded on our own deserts or our own powers for the future but rather much more fully in our God, whose glorious victory in Jesus Christ we share through the life of the Spirit in our hearts. The more we trust and allow God to lead in our lives, the more we will experience true supernatural hope in God painfully in and through, but quite beyond, our own weak powers—an experience at times frightening and emptying but ultimately joyfully exhilarating. St. Paul, in a whole passage from the letter to the Philippians (3:7–14), expresses well the spirit of this conclusion of the formal examen: "I leave the past behind and with hands outstretched to whatever lies ahead I go straight for the goal" (3:13).

Examen and Discernment

We will close this article with some summary remarks about the examen, as here described, and discernment of spirits. When examen is understood in this light and so practiced each day, then it becomes so much more than just a brief exercise performed once or twice a day and that is quite secondary to our formal prayer and active living of God's love in our daily situation. Rather, it becomes an exercise that so focuses and renews our specific faith identity that we should be even more reluctant to omit our examen than our formal contemplative prayer each day. This seems to have been St. Ignatius's view of the practice of the examen. He never talks of omitting it, though he does talk of adapting and abbreviating the daily meditation for various reasons. For him, it seems the examen was central and quite inviolate. This strikes us as strange until we revamp our understanding of the examen. Then perhaps we begin to see the examen as so intimately connected to our growing identity and so important to our finding God in all things at all times that it becomes our central daily experience of prayer.

For Ignatius, finding God in all things is what life is all about. Near the end of his life, he said that "whenever he wished, at whatever hour, he could find God" (*Autobiography,* #99). This is the mature Ignatius, who had so fully allowed God to possess every ounce of his being through a clear, abandoning yes that radiated from the very core of his being that he could be conscious at any moment he wanted of the deep peace, joy, and contentment (consolation, see the *Exercises,* #316) that was the experience of God at the center of his heart. Ignatius's identity, at this point in his life, was quite fully and clearly "in Christ," as Paul says: "For now my place is in him, and I am not dependent upon any of the self-achieved righteousness of the Law" (Philippians 3:9). Ignatius knew and was his true self in Christ.

Being able to find God whenever he wanted, Ignatius was now able to find that God of love in all things through a test for congruence of any interior impulse, mood, or feeling with his true self. Whenever he found interior consonance (which registers as peace, joy, contentment) from the immediate interior movement and felt himself being his true, congruent self, then he knew he had heard God's word to him at that instant. And he responded with that fullness of humble courage so typical of Ignatius. If he discovered interior dissonance, agitation, and disturbance "at the bottom of the heart" (to be carefully distinguished from repugnance "at the top of the head"[2]) and could not find his true congruent self in Christ, then he recognized the interior impulse as an "evil spirit" and he experienced God by "going against" the desolate impulse (cf. the *Exercises,* #319). In this way, he was able to find God in all things by carefully discerning all his interior experiences ("spirits"). Thus discernment of spirits became a daily, very practical living of the art of loving God with his whole heart, whole body, and whole strength. Every moment of life was loving (finding) God in the existential situation in a deep, quiet peace and joy.

For Ignatius, this finding God in the present interior movement, feeling, or option was almost instantaneous in his mature years because the central "feel" or "bent" of his being had so been grasped by God. For the beginner, what was almost instantaneous for the mature Ignatius may require the effort of a prayerful process of a few hours or days, depending on the importance of the movement-impulse to be discerned. In some of his writings, Ignatius uses *examen* to refer to this almost instantaneous test for congruence with his true self—something he could do a number of times every hour of the day. But he also speaks of examen in the formal restricted sense of two quarter-hour exercises of prayer a day.

The intimate and essential relationship between these two senses of examen has been the point of this whole article.

Notes

1. David Asselin, S.J., "Christian Maturity and Spiritual Discernment," *Review for Religious,* 27 (1968): 594.

2. John Carroll Futrell, S.J., *Ignatian Discernment* (St. Louis: Institute of Jesuit Sources, 1970), 64.

"A Check on Our Availability: The Examen"

In an earlier issue (January 1972, "Consciousness Examen") I wrote about a renewed understanding of the traditional Ignatian exercise of the daily examen. In that article, I preferred to talk of an "examen of consciousness" because most of us had come to understand "conscience" in a narrowly moralistic sense. This had turned the examen into a fairly negative practice, soon discarded when we got into the typically busy apostolic life. To set aside specific time each day to see what we did wrong was not very much help. Nor did the practice enrich our apostolate much, because it gradually turned God into Someone always catching us doing something wrong—and thus wreaked havoc on our self-esteem. A good sense of self-value, an effective apostolate, and our image of God are always intimately connected.

A Positive Understanding of the Examen

The formal examen should rather be a time of prayer about how much God has loved me in the very existential details of my day and how that love could have blessed me even more in certain situations if my inner spiritual decisiveness and external presence had been a bit different. This is not just a different articulation of the meaning of the examen. Rather, it leads to an enormous difference attitudinally and effectively. A healthy self-esteem has to be ultimately and irrevocably rooted in God's love, climaxed in the victory in Jesus. This neither excessively highlights, nor denies, my daily sinful weakness. Rather it leads to a consoling humiliation, found in God's forgiveness, which is constantly available in Jesus as my personal savior. In this way, the daily effect of my sinful condition is not to tear down self-worth but to build up true apostolic humility, which itself is the source of genuine self-esteem.

This positive understanding of the examen helps avoid another fallacy. Many times the full, rich prayer of the consciousness examen shrinks into a quick, superficial reflection on the day, and the five traditional elements of the examen thus collapse into the third element by itself—a general survey of the day's activities. The formal examen, however, was never intended to be just a quick reflection on the day. It is supposed to be prayer—and that within a fairly specific form, one related to daily contemplation but not identical to it. And if the examen is to be chiefly about God's love for me, then gratitude should play a major affective role. Of course, it is the gratitude of sinners who are at peace with the fact that they can do nothing on their own, because they are still wonderfully learning how a dear God's love turns everything to good—even their own sinfulness.

The Examen Is Essential to Availability

In the conclusion of his letter to the Society of Jesus on "apostolic availability," Father General Pedro Arrupe made this statement:

> To become partly immobile through lack of availability on the part of individuals and the consequent fear of superiors to give them the missions called for by our apostolate today, would constitute a most serious threat to the very existence of our vocation. . . . Ignatian availability is the guarantee and the *conditio sine qua non* of our practice, which leads to salvation, and alone is of interest to the Society and the Church.

A strong claim!

My central point here is that the daily examen is the *primary* means to maintain this disposition of Ignatian and, indeed, of all apostolic availability. Even so, why should a brief period of prayer assume such great importance? This leads us to another insight often neglected in the past.

The *formal* examen-prayer, with its five elements, (usually) lasting about a quarter-hour, is always a means to the *informal* examen, which is a special faith-sensitivity that is with us all through the day. Often in our early years, we turned the formal examen-prayer into an end in itself, giving to it a rigid fidelity that corrupted its significance. Of course, it would be illusory to imagine that we can grow into living the informal examen-sensitivity without the early development of habitual practice of the formal examen and a continuing adaptation of our involvement with this type of daily prayer.

Through the informal examen, a person acquires a special ability for discerning (or examining) "presence" in everything. For Ignatius, this quality-presence was more important and extensive than the formal examen-prayer, inasmuch as this presence helps the person to recognize the grace of apostolic availability and flexibility that is being offered in every situation. Apostolic availability is a profound faith-experience that roots our identity and security in God's love. When our security is too rooted in a job or a place, or even a certain reputation, there results a stubborn rigidity that undermines our availability, just as availability can equally be undermined by a disordered need for change and variety—as when we are so superficially committed that we really don't care whether we are changed or where we are assigned.

In that same letter, Father Arrupe pointed out some of the challenges for what we have termed *apostolic availability* that are especially present in the new directions, institutional involvements, and types of service that are required in the modern world. What is fundamental, though, is that availability is primarily a readiness and sensitivity of heart, not simply a changing of job and/or place. In the heart of a person who has served for many years in the same mission there can be an availability that is very apostolic and invigorating—and often more difficult than the "availability" that leads to a new assignment. Apostolic availability and genuine perseverance in the same task or place can never be opposed.

In the formal examen, we hold up our day to be seen against the light of God's love. Sometimes this will be more instructive for us than was the experience itself. We may appreciate what we didn't even see in the actual experience.

At other times, we can savor the depths implicit in our sensitivity in the actual experience of the day. The continuing informal examen makes us sensitive in every situation to God's love, which is always available and makes us ready to respond in filial love, as Jesus was—especially on Calvary.

At such a point of insight, we see how often our cowardice or disordered desires reveal us to be persons of the "Second Class" (the *Spiritual Exercises,* #154), who seek to make God come to what we desire. This is precisely backwards: consolation and greater apostolic service are to be found in our coming to what God desires. The sensitivity of apostolic availability distinguishes the heart of a person of the "Third Class" from one of the "Second Class." The difference can become very subtle in one's interior affective life, but what is always at issue is nothing less than better service for the justice of God's kingdom.

Availability and Discernment

In our sinful human condition, apostolic availability does not at all come naturally to us but often is born of our decisive dealing with desolation in accordance with the principles of Ignatian discernment. The seven capital sins, as inner affective experiences (before we intentionally act on them), are each a type of desolate violence endemic to our sinful condition. They infringe on and restrict the freedom of our availability. In decisively going against this desolate violence (see the *Exercises,* #319), we become interiorly available to God's loving and consoling attractiveness, which always frees us for whatever the Holy Spirit is moving us to now. In this way, Jesus' own decisive availability to God, in service to our world, is gradually born in our affectivity through our careful living, with all the subtlety of discernment, in the face of our inner, desolate violence. The daily examen is the most practical and regular means to practice this discernment for availability.

Our *particular* examen could then focus on the flaw or weakness that now is most keeping us from this fuller apostolic availability.

What is that flaw or weakness? It is not so much something that we decide on but rather what God will reveal in the desire that all of us be more and more available to the transforming work of the Holy Spirit in our world. By responding to this call through the particular examen and directing our attention and effort primarily against that flaw or weakness, we are allowing ourselves to be drawn more into the apostolic availability of Jesus, where he and we together best find God.

The Examen: An Action-Reflection Model

Apostolic renewal is not simply being able to get more done. Apostolic activity is not measured simply in quantity but must respond to the dictates of a wise sensitivity in the zealous lover of God. A certain degree of reflectivity is essential to the growth of this sensitivity. Although in the beginning this reflectivity may seem labored and artificial, as one matures in the Spirit it becomes more integrated, less obvious, and part of the "presence" one has everywhere.

There is much talk about various action-reflection models to help renew our apostolic presence, and indeed, some such model can be an essential instrument and method for the formation of apostles. I suggest that the examen is precisely such an action-reflection instrument, one that is built right into our daily life and is capable of fostering apostolic availability as a whole way of life open to service of the needs of our world for God's greater glory.

In these models we reflect on our experience, hoping that the reflection will lead us to better quality in our apostolic efforts. Hence the reflection is never for itself, nor is it directed to a self-centered sanctification. Often in the past, the examen did not have an apostolic orientation but tended to a suffocating introspection. As we mature in our practice of the examen, the separate steps of action-reflection-action integrate into a sensitivity of presence in the activity that makes us available in everything for the call of God's love, in the greater glory of Jesus throughout our world.

Just as the routine and regularity of the daily order help to keep monastic people attuned to God, so the examen can keep apostles, who are actively non-monastic, attuned to God's love and available for a faithful service that is always both response to and union with a God of love, beautifully revealed in Jesus for the transformation of the whole universe.

"Consciousness Examen: Becoming God's Heart for the World"

To live contemplatively, indeed, to become whom we contemplate: this is the invigorating experience, the hallmark enterprise and adventure that human existence is all about—that for which every human heart is longing. The magnetic appeal of the wholly beloved invites our hearts to a transformation that is never easy. But it is so intimately renewing as to be almost irresistible. It is the very heart of love. Lovers in their mutual contemplation are not always explicitly aware of this process of self-transformation into which they are being swept up. But certain challenging moments can starkly reveal the risky loss of self that is involved. And yet the very attractiveness of the beloved provides conviction and motivation to embrace this risk. In that magnetic moment, love seems an opportunity not to be missed. But love's opportunity and risk are also costly—and lovers finally know this. Indeed, the cost involved in the contemplation of lovers strikes to the profound level of self-identity. But cost what it may, the beloved's attractiveness lures the lover on to surprising new depths.

The beloved in our reflection here is Christ Jesus, our God and Lord, our Brother, and, finally, all our sisters and brothers, especially the most suffering ones across all time and space (see Matthew 25:31–46). And contemplative transformation into this beloved is the fundamental process involved in—indeed it *is*—devotion to the Sacred Heart of Jesus Christ. It is also the process with which examination of conscience is concerned. And there we have at once the premise and the product of this reflection.

Both devotion to the Sacred Heart and examination of conscience have a long history in the Ignatian tradition. But they have rarely, if ever, been viewed in relationship to each other. In this article, I will try to show how regular examination of conscience facilitates a transforming experience of one's own heart into the beloved of one's heart, the Sacred Heart of God in Jesus Christ. After a brief summary of the contemporary renewed understanding of the examen, I will make use especially of some of the graces prayed for in the First Week of the Spiritual Exercises in order to describe the continuing conversion involved in a regular practice of examen. Finally, in support of the claim that the examen can convert our hearts into devotion to the Sacred Heart of God, I will describe a little of the apostolic power, the ardent love and thirst for justice, of such a growing and ongoing conversion. Ongoing, for we are never done with love.

In recent years there have been attempts, both within the Jesuit heritage and within the whole church, to renew the understanding and practice of examination of conscience and of devotion to the Sacred Heart. Examination of conscience is now more often called consciousness examen or awareness examen.[1] In its renewed form, the examen continues to bless the hearts of many busy believers and sensitize them to the loving presence of God in all of daily life. And while much work has been done in developing a contemporary understanding of devotion to the Sacred Heart,[2] perhaps the actual practice of the devotion is not so widespread as that of consciousness examen, or at least it is not widespread among those who frequently make use of consciousness examen. This article, finally, though its central point is to relate the two practices, is concerned more with the personal effects of regular examen than it is with the details of traditional or recent developments in devotion to the Sacred Heart.

Renewed Understanding of the Examen

In the renewed understanding of the examen, two insights are key. First, a much more positive perspective has corrected a past view that often deteriorated into an overly negative, moralistic misunderstanding. Rather than highlighting the bad actions of a day, the examen gives primary concern to what is primary: God's revelation, a steadfast love in Christ Jesus always inviting and invigorating our consciousness. Formal examen sensitizes our hearts to the presence of this love in the ordinary details of every day. Whenever this love is recognized and responded to, our hearts simply must come alive with joy and gratitude. So gratitude is the major element in the actual time of examen-prayer, as it should also be in our daily lives of faith. This gratefulness for the wonder of God's love stirs hearts to action. And so gratitude becomes the chief motive from which all ministry pours.

As the examen begins to make our hearts more aware of God's perduring love, we also begin to recognize how often and how easily we can be oblivious to that love or how subtly, yet quite stubbornly, we can refuse to respond to love. This realization, when faced honestly and not rationalized away, can, whether rudely or quietly, awaken our hearts with healthy guilt, with sorrow and repentance. As this article will develop later, this experience of guilt and sorrow is anything but pleasant, yet as an experience of God's love, it does purify us it does transform us. And the effect of that can only be a bolder, freer, more wide-ranging apostolic service. Mature faith and discipleship cannot happen without this painful transformation in the humiliating experience of guilt and sorrow. As the repentant sinner encounters God's forgiveness in Jesus, sorrow is transformed into hopeful, vigorous gratitude—and a burning zeal to serve God's loving justice in our world. In this way, thanksgiving—the central driving force in the heart of any mature disciple of Jesus Christ—dominates the daily examen and fuels its impulse toward loving action.

A second insight that renews our understanding of the exa-men is the importance of the *informal* examen, as distinguished from, though obviously not unrelated to, the *formal* examen.[3] The formal examen is a specific time and style of prayer. In a previous article I described the five traditional elements of such prayer.[4] Never meant as an end in itself, this formal practice of examen should gradually spill over and infiltrate, as a special faith-sensitivity, a person's daily life. And so we come upon the informal examen: a way of living. The informal examen is more a matter of who we are and who we are becoming, whereas the formal examen is a

GEORGE A. ASCHENBRENNER, S.J.

specific prayer we regularly practice. Thus a regular practice of examen can lead to that self-transformation that makes possible a genuine faith-sensitivity of heart, a dynamic connaturality with the Beloved, which we are calling here *informal examen*. This dynamic development of formal examen into informal, into a pervasive faith-sensitivity of heart, is crucial—crucial both to a proper understanding of examen itself and to its role in the human heart's deeply desired experience of love: our becoming whom we contemplate.

Daily Conversion in Faith

Jesus' ministry erupts publicly among the people in a great sense of urgency: a wholly new revelation of God's love and the need for reform of mind and heart, if one is to recognize and respond to that love. It is so clear at the beginning of Mark and in the synagogue scene of chapter four in Luke. This radical personal conversion of faith is often described in the Scriptures as a matter of repentance. As a conversion that will cost a whole life-time, it continually involves the risking and sacrificing of a temptingly attractive but false, illusory self while a radically true and radiantly new creation is born in a person's daily response to the quiet urgency of God's love. But no experience of merely passing excitement will suffice for this.

Nor can such repentance and radical change of outlook ever be reduced simply to our own planning and control. A strategy of clear-sighted tactics and fierce determination will always prove futile all by itself. In fact, if not properly motivated and accompanied by grace, it can actually corrupt the very adventure of faith into something unwholesome and unholy. Without a genuine experience of the wonder of God's love, the gospel call, the call by grace and favor to radical change, cannot be heard, and healthy repentance cannot happen.[5] It is the attractive beauty and power of God's love that reveals the inadequacy and sinfulness of our condition and unloosens in our hearts a desire to be much more than what we now may be. It is in this way that the wonder of God's love reveals our sinfulness. And this profound truth, so capable of being misunderstood, is always the bedrock of mature spiritual life. God alone sees our sinfulness most clearly for what it truly is: a choice against love. And it is this God who calls us to intimacy in the beautiful revelation of Jesus come among us as forgiveness. Every detail of Jesus' life, most especially his dramatic experience on Calvary, stretches and stirs our hearts in hope for a new creation, a new life, a whole new self. But repentance, with its purifying pain and suffering, is the only way to this urgently longed-for newness.

An honest repentant acknowledgement of sinfulness in the face of such love is neither obvious nor easy, because it makes us conscious of humiliation. The guilt and shame and the embarrassment that come in the wake of such an acknowledgement sting and singe our consciousness. In the presence of such love, they make our spirits blush. The pain and hurt will, most often, and quite spontaneously, make us wary and seek to activate defense mechanisms such as the rationalizations of denial and the distractions, not of joy, but of pleasure. These are moments for careful discernment in the life of any believer. For the humiliating pain of acknowledged sin, as intended here, is not the result of some overly scrupulous conscience. Nor is it the unhealthy guilt of self-hatred. Rather, it is the purifying consolation—not desolation, but consolation, however scouring—the consoling experience of God calling us to greater love and life and faith. Despite the pain, therefore, this repentant blush of heart is a grace not to be rejected. It is essential to any mature faith, to any measured zeal for God's world, to any discipleship that hopes to brave the road's full distance.

The guilt that introduces our embarrassed, repentant response to God's great, tender love requires a brief description here. Much past experience of unhealthy guilt has understandably provoked the overreaction to, even to the point of a dangerous disregard of, all guilt as if all guilt were unhealthy. Though unhealthy guilt can surely plague and dishearten us, there is a guilt born of God, and it stings. But for the lover, it also signals the Beloved's presence, a very active presence, a redemptive consciousness, inviting greater intimacy in faith with God. Unhealthy guilt is always anxious,

GEORGE A. ASCHENBRENNER, S.J.

worried about self, in excessive fear of punishment, preoccupied with failure, at times verging on despair in the face of some unrealistic perfectionism. But healthy, consoling guilt is always the result of an interpersonal love relationship. And it focuses the heart beyond the self, on the Beloved, in painful sorrow for the wound one's lack of love has caused. Healthy guilt does not despair, nor does it disrupt the deepest peace of the soul. The reason for this is that healthy guilt is always intimately and very positively related to encounter, a repentant sinner's encounter with God's forgiveness revealed and available now in a crucified Son's intransigent love.

In the Dying, a New Life

But in the tense struggle of this inner guilt, shame, and sorrow, we usually become aware of the risk and high stakes involved. A self, or some aspect of a self with which we have been enamored, perhaps for a long time, must be let go. Something must die if the new is to be born. It is a mortifying experience, but as it is not a mortification simply of our own making, neither can the outcome of it be clearly grasped in advance. It is a moment of perceived high risk. And the helplessness of such a moment, when we are on the verge of letting go of what used to be and are not yet in possession of what will be, can profoundly daunt and agitate our spirit. Furthermore, it is in no way simply our own power and ingenuity that will create a different future. In the helpless and sorrowful awareness of our sinfulness, it is only an act of trusting abandonment of self, sometimes done in the dark aloneness of faith, that will allow the Beloved to gift us with God's holiness, our only true human future. A process of conversion that has begun in love leads now to even greater love as a beloved God, in that faithful promise that is the risen Jesus, defies all darkness and rejects absurdity and pain as the final word, whether about this world or the next.

The heart of God revealed in Jesus excites our hearts with the invitation to a new and brighter future. But only a heart scoured clean in the humiliation of repentance can respond to that invitation. The issue is as profound as self-transformation and as hopeful as a wholly new creation. But without a mortified response to God's loving invitation and without a risky letting go of self, such a future remains simply tantalizing, a cheap grace, an illusion.

The forgiving love of God brings the process of repentance to a conclusion of lively gratitude, profound joy, and enthusiastic zeal for ministry. The sorrow of a forgiven sinner is not depressing, however painfully purifying. Neither is this sorrow obliterated by the joyous gratitude and zeal for service that realized forgiveness brings. Rather, the humble, saved sinner, while not destructively focused on the past, never simply forgets the sorrowful memory of forgiven sin. One cannot help but wonder whether Peter, in the maturity of his joy, during his after-breakfast walk with the risen Jesus, did not once again feel his eyes well up with tears as three awkward questions burned his soul with his own lonely truth but burned it precisely for the sake of fidelity, the journey in companionship, and yes, for the great holiness that lay ahead for Peter (John 21:15–19).

The new self created in God's forgiveness is always strongly characterized by a profound, joyful thanksgiving for a deed neither deserved nor capable of accomplishment on one's own. This deed of forgiveness and the hope of a new and better future resonate strongly in the repentant sinner's heart, now riveted on the challenging beauty of God's forgiving love, found fleshed forever in Jesus on the cross. And so the whole dynamic of the First Week of the Spiritual Exercises propels a person to confrontation, to enlightenment and encouragement before this passionate experience of Jesus on Calvary. Having taken upon himself the sins of all, this Son, anguished in an olive grove over the agonizing prospect of a humiliating death, is able to renew that trusting abandonment of self that allows him to find once again, as always, not previous to but in the very abandonment of dying, his dear Father. And his beloved Father blesses this anguished abandonment with a future of absolute fullness in resurrection. In the fact of such enlivening abandonment on Jesus' part, we can find the graceful encouragement needed for that surrender of self that repentance always demands.

GEORGE A. ASCHENBRENNER, S.J.

It is at this moment that the graces of fidelity and perseverance take root in the forgiven sinner's experience. And so Jesus' death into the future of resurrection stands faithfully, for all ages, as God's forgiveness. It gives graceful encouragement to all repentant sinners in this risky and humiliating process of self-transformation. The persevering faithfulness of this new creation, this new heart, will always depend on how profoundly, how pervasively transformed the repentant sinner is in the encounter with God's Word of forgiveness.

As we gaze on God's forgiveness in Jesus crucified, besides a lively gratitude and profound joy, our heart knows the expansiveness of a great desire for God in Jesus—an apostolic desire to give ourselves as Jesus did in the ministry of God's forgiving justice. This desire at the end of the First Week continues to expand as the attractiveness of God's love in Jesus is revealed through the remaining weeks of the Exercises. God's Spirit and kingdom, revealed so compellingly in Jesus, become our wholehearted desire. To live in daily imitation of Jesus, to serve as an apostle in whatever way God desires, becomes the very energy of our hearts. And yet, as the experience continues, this desire can stretch our hearts still further: we may be so transformed and, in such transformation, so intimately identified with Jesus that we become and, in the thoroughly real way that the mysticism of baptism and Eucharist accomplish in us, may *be* Jesus in and for our world. And so the joyous thanksgiving of a forgiven sinner, so much more than a mere devotional satisfaction, sets our hearts afire with such desire for new identity in Christ Jesus that we become mystical activists, heralds everywhere of the good news of God's transforming forgiveness.

This reflection offers the view that consciousness examen may play a role of special importance in facilitating such a process of radical conversion. The profundity and pervasiveness of the transformation spoken of will depend in large measure on a regular practice of examen. And rather than putting a clear conclusion to the process of radical conversion, the Exercises provide enlightening direction for the further and continual deepening of desire for this daily identification with Jesus. For this reason, as the formal Exercises conclude and move to become daily life, we are always left with an even greater need than before for regular examen, that we may continue the daily discernment of God's love converting us steadily into Christ Jesus, our Lord.

Goal of Examen: Devotion to the Sacred Heart of God in Jesus

Long after the retreat experience of the Exercises is finished, regular examen keeps our hearts sensitive and responsive to the attractiveness of the Sacred Heart of God in Jesus. As we have already seen, thanksgiving and sorrow are the two chief affections in faith of the examen—and the sorrow itself, as we have also seen, finds its fulfillment in thanksgiving. And so it is in and through its term of thanksgiving that regular examen mediates our conversion and growth into Christ Jesus. Through the basic thrust of the examen, each believer becomes a concrete embodiment here and now of the Sacred Heart of God in Jesus. Consciousness examen, therefore, by facilitating the transformation whereby a serious believer and disciple becomes devoted to the Sacred Heart, is profoundly related to that same devotion. For in this sense of the word, *devotion* refers to the fundamental orientation of a believing heart to the heart of God in Christ Jesus. And this sense of devotion cuts far beneath—not necessarily denying but rather rooting—any specific, traditional devotional details and practices.

The transformation of self whereby our hearts radically become devoted to the Sacred Heart accomplishes some perceptible results in our lives. Growing integrity of heart, wholeheartedness, and Ignatian magnanimity gradually center, unite, and identify our whole person and presence in the world. A white inner stillness, fanned to burning flame in God's own creative love, radiates an energy of recollection—a collectedness—that can meld our often fragmentary faith into the strong, living organism of a life decisively for God.

Such wholeheartedness first gives enlightenment, then courage, toward a fundamental desire and choice in the direction of the "heavenly" things of consolation and away from the "earthly"

GEORGE A. ASCHENBRENNER, S.J.

things of desolation. These desolate, "earthly" things live in our flesh as the seven capital, selfish impulses toward sin that the Christian tradition has known so well for centuries; whereas the "heavenly" things of God's consoling love are the opposite impulses that also live in our consciousness, where the Spirit of Jesus invites and breathes their confirmation, their development in us, as virtues, as the very shape of our heart. In the interweaving complexity and tangle of our daily consciousness, we discover that the tempting experience of these capital impulses to sin is precisely the battle-field upon which the fidelity of our commitment and devotion to the virtuous heart of God in Christ is tested and strengthened. And so it is usually by standing strong against the tempting intensity of lust that the virtue of chastity grows. It is by decisively acknowledging and carefully standing against the violence of desolate rage that the tensile strength of gentleness is forged. And so of all the personal and communal motions of spirit that impel us toward or away from the justice of the Reign of God. The examen is daily involvement in this process of transforming the impulsive desolations of our consciousness into the deep, consoling devotion and virtue of God's Sacred Heart. Once again, as described earlier in this article, we notice that it is precisely in the dying that the new is born. And what is newly born through these mortifying struggles on the inner battlefield of our hearts—the heart of each of us and the communal, societal heart of each group, each social structure—always affects apostolic presence in the world, always decisively affects actions for or against God's justice as revealed in the loving Heart of Jesus.

Finally, this conversion into the Sacred Heart of God in Jesus, this process of our becoming devotion to the Sacred Heart, does not replace our weakness with an arrogant sense of our own strength. No, just the opposite! Maturity in faith is always growth to grateful realization both of our weakness and of our dependence on God's love for everything. A steadfast belief in God's love does not replace human weakness. Rather, it helps us to wait patiently upon the Lord and recognize and celebrate God's love bringing strength into our weakness. For God's power is at its best in our weakness (see 2 Corinthians 12:7–10). It is a power that is needed, for becoming whom we contemplate takes courage, even as it brings energy for it. It is high adventure, with a promised wage of persecution, to enter and be taken up into the affectivity of Jesus, God's countercultural heart for the world.

Consciousness examen, then, is not a way to greater, self-reliant strength. But as its daily practice transforms us into the Sacred Heart, we may become whom we contemplate and so stand in this world as living witnesses, agents of love, inviting others into God's Heart in Christ Jesus: "Come to me, all you who labor and are overburdened, and I will give you rest. Shoulder my yoke and learn from me, for I am gentle and humble in heart, and you will find rest for your souls. Yes, my yoke is easy and my burden light" (Matthew 11:28–30).

And one more time we listen to the Beloved, becoming whom we contemplate: "This text is being fulfilled, today, even as you listen". (Luke 4:21)

> The spirit of the Lord has been given to me, for he has anointed me. He has sent me to bring the good news to the poor, to proclaim liberty to captives and to the blind new sight, to set the downtrodden free, to proclaim the Lord's year of favor. (Luke 4:18–19)

Through a companionship with Jesus made intimate and tender, strong and apostolically peremptory; through days and years of fidelity to the examen of consciousness; and through the dynamic energy continually released in the experience of forgiven sinfulness, we may come to the apostolic gift that the faithful friends of God can know. In becoming whom we contemplate, we may devoutly, reverently, boldly, and with the divine thirst itself for justice become, each of us and together, in the Holy Spirit, God's own heart for the world.

Notes

1. George Aschenbrenner, S.J., "Consciousness Examen," *Review for Religious* (January 1972): 14–21. See also the lengthy, very helpful article of David Keith Townsend, S.J., "The Examen Re-examined," *CIS* 18, 2 (1987): 11–64.

2. Annice Callahan, R.S.C.J., *Karl Rahner's Spirituality of the Pierced Heart: A Reinterpretation of Devotion to the Sacred Heart* (New York: University Press of America, 1985). This book contains references to the essential texts of Rahner on this subject.

3. George Aschenbrenner, S.J., "A Check on Our Availability: The Examen," *Review for Religious* (May 1980): 321–4.

4. Aschenbrenner, "Consciousness Examen," 14–21.

5. See my article "Forgiveness," *Sisters Today* 45 (1973): 185–92.